FLIGHT WITH POWER

FLIGHT WITH POWER

POWER

THE FIRST TEN YEARS
DAVID WRAGG

BE.2

ST. MARTIN'S PRESS

Also by David Wragg

World's Air Forces
A Dictionary of Aviation
Speed in the Air
Flight Before Flying

For Sally

My wife, who married aeroplanes as well!

Library of Congress Catalog Card Number: 78-69740
First published in the United States of America in 1979

ISBN: 0-312-29630-4

CONTENTS

INTRODUCTION

Several thousand years elapsed after the first attempts at flight before lighter-than-air flight became possible, and another 120 years passed before this could be complemented with powered heavier-than-air flight. Following this break-through it was the work of just a few decades before flying became an everyday event, regardless of light or darkness, and possible in all but the very worst weather conditions. As the aeroplane grew up, reaching high speeds and capable of flying at considerable altitudes, it became too large for the individual entrepreneur, and indeed frequently an undertaking for several manufacturers assisted by govern-ments. In contrast, the first ten years or so of powered, heavier-than-air flight rested solely upon the individuals con-cerned, giving aviation a degree of human involvement seldom repeated after the start of World War I, and certainly lost altogether after the end of World War II.

Flight with Power: The First Ten Years takes the story of flying through the first exciting decade of powered, but heavier-than-air, flying, starting with the historic first flight by Orville Wright on 17 December 1903, and ending with the British Empire and Germany at war on 4 August 1914. The period was one of trial and error, and aviators were largely pre-occupied with the need first for recognition and then for acceptance of the aeroplane. As always, there were the tragedies and the successes, but at this time the outstanding characteristic was the importance of the pioneer aviator, the first in the air!

As always, I am in debt to those who have kindly assisted with the provision of material for this book, including Miss Florence Vaughan of the Science Museum, London, Mr E. Hine of the Imperial War Museum, Mr E.E. Stott of the Royal Aircraft Establishment, Farnborough, Jim White of Short Brothers & Harland, Jerry Kearns of the Library of Congress, Lt-Col. J.B. Reveilhac of the Musée de l'Air, Paris, Mrs A. Naylor of the Royal Aeronautical Society, and Times News-papers, without all of whom this book could hardly have been written.

David W. Wragg

1
THE WRIGHTS LEAD THE WAY

First aeroplane flights, Langley, Jatho, Archdeacon, Ferber, Esnault-Pelterie, Voisin, Blériot, the FAI

'I wish to invite very special attention to the wonderful advance made in aviation by the brothers Wright. I have every confidence in their uprightness, and in the correctness of their statements. It is a fact that they have flown and operated personally a flying machine for a distance of over three miles, at a speed of 35mph.'
Colonel J.E. Capper
(1905)

O n 1 January 1905, the apiarists of America opened their respected journal, *Gleanings in Bee Culture*, to read:

It was my privilege, on the 20th day of September, 1904, to see the first successful trip of an airship, without balloon to sustain it, that the world has ever made, that is, to turn the corners and come back to the starting point. When it first turned that circle, and came near to the starting point, I was right in front of it; and I said then, and I believe still, it was one of the grandest sights, if not the grandest sight, of my life. Imagine a locomotive that has left its track and is climbing up in the air right toward you – a locomotive without any wheels, we will say, but with white wings instead. Well now, imagine this white locomotive, with wings that spread 20 feet each way, coming right toward you with a tremendous flap of its propellers, and you will have something like what I saw. The younger brother bade me move to one side for fear it might come down suddenly; but I tell you, friends, the sensation that one feels in such a crisis is something hard to describe.

This was nothing less than the first published eye-witness account of an aeroplane flight, and its author, Amos Root, the owner-editor of *Gleanings in Bee Culture*, was making journalistic as well as aeronautical history with his account of the Wright Flyer II flying the first circle. Whether the event ranked as apiaristic history as well must be open to question, but one can only hope that the readers of the *Gleanings* forgave the intrusion of a different variety of winged being.

The general cynicism about powered, heavier-than-air flight which had hitherto been shared by the press as a whole had meant that no reporters accepted the invitations issued by the Wright Brothers to attend the first flight on 17 December 1903, and statements and reports to the press had been ignored. On the two occasions when journalists had gone to see the Wrights, mechanical faults or inclement weather had prevented flight from taking place, and the visitors left with their prejudices intact. Only Root

had shown any real open-mindedness, not to say persistence.

It would be wrong to assume that the Wright brothers had worked completely without public and scientific recognition. Their glider flights, conducted from 1900 to 1902, first at Kitty Hawk on the North Carolina coast, and then at the nearby Kill Devil Hills, had attracted a good deal of attention in the United States and in Europe. Much of this was due to the activities of their friend and self-appointed publicist, the retired railway engineer and gliding pioneer Octave Chanute, who had attached himself to the two young bicycle-manufacturers from Dayton, Ohio, in 1900. To the extent that the brothers had studied his work, *Progress in Flying Machines*, published in 1894, at the start of their researches, Chanute was also something of a mentor to the Wrights.

French interest in their gliding experiments was such that Chanute had been able to address a dinner of the Aéro Club de France on 2 April 1903, describing the

The historic photograph of the flight that started it all! Orville takes off in the Wright Flyer I on 17 December 1903, as Wilbur stands by, having steadied the aircraft's wing during the take-off run. The aircraft flew in a 27mph headwind, and the flight lasted just 12 seconds, covering 120 feet, although this would have been further had the wind dropped.

Wilbur Wright, the elder of the two brothers and the prime mover in their interest in aeronautics – photographed while in France with the Wright A biplane in 1908. Wilbur died early from typhoid fever in 1912, although by that time the Wrights had passed the pinnacles of their success, and were failing to keep abreast of developments.

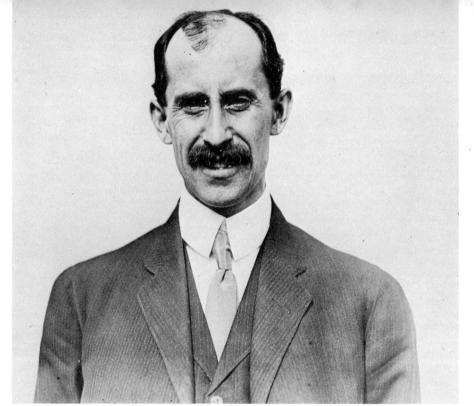

Orville Wright, the younger brother, who made the first flight, the first passenger-carrying flights, and was involved in the first fatal aeroplane accident, suffering injury himself, while his passenger was killed after a propeller shattered on their aircraft.

Wright No. 3 glider, and his own work, with the aid of illustrations. This moved one member of his audience, Ernest Archdeacon (1863–1957), to form an Aviation Committee of the Aéro Club de France, with the declared intention of beating the Wright brothers in the race to achieve powered, heavier-than-air flight!

A leading member of the Aéro Club de France, with an interest in aeronautical development which was both philanthropic and nationalistic, Archdeacon encouraged a young member of the Club, Robert Esnault-Pelterie (1881–1957) to design a 'Wright-type' glider. This failed, because Esnault-Pelterie misunderstood the Wright principles of control in roll. Yet another French aeronaut, Captain Ferdinand Ferber (1862–1909) produced 'une réproduction de l'appareil Wright', based on the Wright No. 3 glider, with the aid of Gabriel Voisin (1880–1973), although this did not become airborne until 1904, and lacked any form of control in roll.

Mundane although it may sound this attitude to the question of control in roll effectively separated the bird-men from the boys with kites! On the one hand, there were those who recognised that to be

successful an aeroplane had to be freely manoeuvrable in three dimensions. The Wright brothers were among these. On the other, there were those who possessed what has since become known as the 'chauffeur mentality' and saw the aircraft travelling on the air very much as a car or a boat moves across the earth's surface. Those holding to this theory believed in inherent stability for aircraft design, but while this worked well for unmanned models, there could be a sudden loss of stability in a crosswind, and directional control was also difficult. The Wright brothers' theory of inherent instability meant that an aeroplane could only be kept flying by the skill of its pilot – but it worked!

Even while experimenting with their gliders, the Wrights had realised that full control could only be achieved by using a combination of rudder and wing-warping, described by the brothers as a 'helical twisting' of the wings; it preceded the aileron in practical use.

There was also a need to distinguish between flight, and powered leaps or hops, in which the force which counted was that of the take-off run. True flight requires that the engine is able to sustain the aircraft's progress through the air.

The flight must also be long enough for control to be exercised by the pilot – the presence of these two factors made the flights of 17 December 1903 different from those of Du Temple, Mozhaiski and Ader which had gone before.

Perhaps no better explanation exists than that of the first true aviator, Orville Wright:

When we rose on the morning of the 17th, the puddles of water, which had been standing about camp since the recent rains, were covered with ice. The wind had a velocity of from 22 to 27 mph. We thought it would die down before long, but when 10 o'clock arrived, and the wind was as brisk as ever, we decided that we had better get the machine out. Wilbur having used his turn on the unsuccessful attempt on the 14th, the right to the first trial belonged to me. Wilbur ran at the side, holding the wing to balance it on the track. The machine, facing a 27 mile wind, started very slowly. Wilbur was able to stay with it until it lifted from the track after a forty-foot run.

The course of the flight up and down was exceedingly erratic. The control of the front rudder was difficult. As a result, the machine would rise suddenly to about ten feet, and then as suddenly dart for the ground. A sudden dart when a little over 120 feet from the point at which it rose into the air, ended the flight.

This flight lasted only twelve seconds, but it was nevertheless the first in the history of the world in which a machine carrying a man raised itself by its own power into the air in full flight, had sailed forward without reduction of speed, and had finally landed at a point as high as that from which it started.

The toss of a coin had given Wilbur the first chance on 14 December, but he pulled the aircraft off the track too

A starboard side view of the Flyer I.

The Flyer I, a view from the front. The twist of the drive chain to the port propeller to provide contra-rotation of the propellers can be seen clearly.

The first real aeroplane engine – built by the Wrights for the Flyer I, and subsequently developed for their other aircraft in the continued absence of lighter or more powerful, reliable powerplants.

sharply, and it stalled before crash-landing in the sand, sustaining slight damage. However, he followed Orville's flight with one of 175 feet, leaving Orville to cover 200 feet on a third flight; finally Wilbur flew 852 feet in 59 seconds, although bearing in mind the strong head-wind this last flight was probably equivalent to one of half-a-mile through the air.

The Wrights' ideas about the true meaning of flight were based on realistic estimates of the potentialities of powered hops. Wilbur once calculated that a powered leap could extend for as much as 250 feet, although experts since have come to consider that a quarter-of-a-mile might be possible.

This approach contrasted with that of the Wrights' main rival at the time, the famous American astronomer, Professor Samuel Pierpoint Langley. Langley was attracted by the idea of the tandem-wing monoplane, pioneered in England by D.S. Brown, whom Langley visited in 1874. On his return to the United States, Langley first experimented with a number of twisted-rubber motor tandem-wing

models, before producing a series of more or less successful steam-powered models, known as 'Aerodromes'. A better publicist than the Wright brothers, Langley succeeded in obtaining a $50,000 United States War Department grant for the construction of a full-sized petrol-engined aircraft. A quarter-scale prototype was built in 1901, but did not fly successfully until mid-1903.

No form of control in roll was provided on the 'Aerodrome A', as the full-sized aircraft was known. A petrol engine, designed and built by his associates, S.M. Balzer and C.M. Manly, powered two pusher-propellers mounted behind the forward wing. The pilot sat in the fuselage, level with the wing, and could move the rudder or control engine speed – and that was about all! Partly because of his advanced years, and possibly not wishing to get the $50,000 wet, Langley left the piloting of the 'Aerodrome A' to the unfortunate Manly. Manly was in the pilot's seat when, on 7 October 1903, the aircraft was catapulted from the roof of Langley's houseboat, moored on the Potomac River. Unlike the Wright brothers' efforts, this attracted press attention, including a notice in *The Times* of London:

Professor Langley's flying machine, which is built without a balloon and

A rival and contemporary of the Wrights, although he fell far short of them in technical knowledge, the American astronomer, Samuel Pierpoint Langley, built the Aerodrome A, in 1903, with the aid of a $50,000 grant from the United States War Department. The photograph shows the aircraft on the roof of Langley's houseboat on the Potomac River, before one of its two unsuccessful catapult launchings.

The Wright Flyer II of 1904, which flew the first circle on 20 September, as well as leading to the first known published eye-witness account of an aeroplane in the air. Unlike their previous experiments, those on the Flyer II were carried out at the Huffman Prairie, near the brothers' home at Dayton.

The first practical aeroplane, the Wright Flyer III, in the air on 12 September 1905, over the Huffman Prairie. The 'III' followed the 'I' and 'II' in having a prone position for the pilot at first, but this was later modified to a sitting position and then provision was made for a passenger to be carried.

for which the Government granted a subvention of £15,000, was launched today from the rails over the float-boat at Whitewater, a section of the Potomac River. The trial was a failure, the machine soon striking the water with the result that it was damaged. Professor Manly, assistant to Professor Langley, was on board, but escaped with a ducking. He explained that the launching was purely experimental, and that the machine behaved perfectly when it started. Previous experiments have been made with models only, and that the trial was the first made with the full-sized airship, which is constructed to carry a passenger.

The same 'experiment' was repeated on 8 December, to give Manly another ducking. Most of the press had lost interest by this time, and this occurrence so near to the Wright brothers' first flights may account for much of the indifference shown.

Meanwhile, a German civil servant of Russian origin, Karl Jatho, built a biplane with a 9hp petrol motor which managed to make a number of hops in August and November 1903. It, too, lacked any adequate means of control.

Against all of this, and the triumph, albeit unheralded and unsung, of the Wright brothers in December 1903, it is odd to note the remarks of Archdeacon, when speaking of the Wright gliders in April 1903. 'Will the homeland of the Montgolfiers,' he asked, 'have the shame of allowing the ultimate discovery of aerial science to be realised abroad?' At the same time Ferber remarked that 'the aeroplane must not be allowed to be perfected in America.'

In September, the British Association for the Advancement of Science, an institution which could count Sir George Cayley amongst its founder members, was told that there had been 'little advance in aeronautics over the past 50 years', i.e. since the Giffard airship of 1852, although promise was held out for Langley's idea.

A more light-hearted note might seem to be struck by a successful trip across the English Channel, from Calais to Dover on the night of 6 and 7 November, by Samuel F. Cody, the inventor of the 'war kite', who travelled in a collapsible kite-boat. However, this event, somewhat reminiscent of Pocock's with the kite-carriage some years earlier, was a serious experiment to judge the value of the kite

While the Wright Brothers were flying powered heavier-than-air machines in the United States, the French were still pre-occupied with the glider. This model, built by Gabriel Voisin for Archdeacon, a moving force behind the Aéro Club de France, combined the work of a number of pioneers, notably Hargrave, the Australian inventor of the box-kite.

Archdeacon started to experiment with his Voisin float-glider on the River Seine in June 1905, being towed off by a motor-boat, which obviously doubled as a rescue craft! Archdeacon is here being taken to the shore after his glider crashed on landing.

for navigational purposes! Not surprisingly, Cody was nearly run down by a steamship, which then tried to rescue him, mistaking his kite for a distress signal. Such was the state of affairs on the eve of the Wright brothers' success. Perhaps their four flights were mundane by comparison with the attempts of Langley and Cody!

While disappointed in the lack of attention accorded their achievement, the Wrights did at least have the consolation of knowing that the flight had been successfully photographed by the pre-set camera, which they had left for a coast-guard to operate. They had not been able to develop the photographs until their return home to Dayton, in time for the Christmas holiday with their elderly father.

They started the New Year busily engaged in designing and building the 'Flyer II' and its motor. A friend and benefactor, Torrence Huffman, a Dayton financier and landowner, lent the brothers a 90-acre field, known locally as the Huffman Prairie, for use as an aerodrome, saving them the time and expense of travelling to the Kill Devil Hills, and the risk of accident to their frail machine while in transit. It was at the Huffman Prairie that the Flyer II made its first flight on 23 May 1904 – the short design and construction period being attributable to the close relationship with the Flyer I. The main differences between the two aircraft were the substitution of a wing camber of 1 in 25 for the 1 in 20 of the original, the use of a 16hp engine with new propellers, and lower gearing to the propellers.

The 'II's flights were also notable for the use of the Wrights' take-off device, which remained in use until 1910 for their own aircraft. This consisted of a tall derrick with a weight attached to a rope, the rope then running down to the starting end of the take-off track, running along to the take-off end and then back to the starting point, where it was attached to the lower wing of the aircraft. A simple, but nonetheless effective device, the pull of the falling weight started the aircraft along the track, assisting the engine in rapidly attaining take-off speed.

During 1904, eighty flights were made with the new aeroplane, the main highlight being Wilbur's first flight in a circle on 20 September, which so impressed Amos Root! Another achievement came on 9 November, when Wilbur undertook the first flight of more than five minutes' duration, making four circuits of the Huffman Prairie and flying for about three miles. Yet, the 'II' was still not a really practical heavier-than-air flying-machine. The brothers had still not overcome its tendency to stall and fall out of control in a tight turn, so that all flights were conducted at low altitude and the turns were the shallowest possible.

The Europeans, with their great ballooning tradition and with the work of Cayley, Pénaud, Lilienthal and Pilcher

Also in June 1905, although a little later than Archdeacon, Louis Blériot took delivery of a Voisin float-glider, seen here before being towed off the River Seine by a motor-boat.

behind them, could manage only tentative gliding flights. In fact, Esnault-Pelterie, Ferber and Archdeacon each built 'Wright-type' gliders, or adaptations of the Wright designs, which were more notable for omissions of design features than for any innovation. True, Esnault-Pelterie did make an attempt to introduce primitive elevons to his glider in October 1904, but he later did much harm to European aviation progress by writing a paper describing wing-warping, which he understood hardly at all, as structurally dangerous.

Real progress continued to be made at Dayton, regardless of European beliefs, but the St Louis Exposition of 1904 did at least provide a meeting place for minds which were rather more open on the subject of the Wrights than those who saw the young Americans only as irritating rivals.

The Wrights had a well-established pattern for designing and building during the winter months, ready for a summer season of trials. The winter of 1904–5 was no exception and by June 1905, they had completed their brilliant Flyer III. This differed from the earlier aircraft by having a reduced wing area and by reverting to the camber of the Flyer I, although wing anhedral was dispensed with entirely, the elevator and rudder were enlarged, and the whole structure strengthened. The Flyer II engine was retained, however. First flight was at Huffman on 23 June, and some forty flights were made by mid-October.

So successful was this aircraft that it has become generally recognised as the first practical aeroplane. Even the problem of stalling while turning was solved – by putting the nose of the aircraft down to increase speed in the turn. A succession of endurance records was established, culminating in a flight of 24.2 miles in

58 minutes on 5 October, which ended only when the aircraft ran out of fuel.

To the citizens of Dayton and the neighbouring farmers around the Huffman Prairie, aeroplane flight was, if not quite an everyday event, still something with an air of the commonplace about it. Yet, the United States Board of Ordnance continued to reject repeated offers by the Wrights to sell the U.S. Government an aircraft, simply stating that the Board was not interested in any aeroplane which had still to be built!

The frustration of dealing with stone-faced officialdom was compounded of very real anxiety over the grant of patents, without which the work of several years was vulnerable, to say the least. In fact, patents were not granted until 1906, by which time the French magazine *L'Aérophile*, had published a fairly comprehensive account of the Wright designs.

The most successful of the Wrights' early contacts with officialdom was with a British Army officer, Colonel J.E. Capper, who was Superintendent of the Government Aircraft Factory, later the Royal Aircraft Factory, at Farnborough in Hampshire. On learning that the Wrights had offered to sell an aircraft to his government, Capper, in the United States for the St Louis Exposition, took the opportunity of meeting the brothers, and also Chanute and Langley. In January 1905, he had been sufficiently impressed to write to the War Office in London:

> I wish to invite very special attention to the wonderful advance made in aviation by the brothers Wright. I have every confidence in their uprightness, and in the correctness of their statements. It is a fact that they have flown and operated personally a flying machine for a distance of over three miles, at a speed of 35mph.

Unfortunately, negotiations with the British War Office were unsuccessful. The War Office would not buy without first seeing a demonstration, but the Wrights, at this time still anxious for their patents, would not show their aircraft to other experts without first receiving an order.

In the face of such discouragement, the Wrights abandoned their experiments at

the end of the 1905 season, and did not undertake further flights during 1906 or 1907, although in the second year they did further design work and tried to apply pressure behind the scenes.

Archdeacon, meanwhile, had built a pilotless glider designed to pave the way for a powered craft, although still lacking any means of control in roll. Towed off a wooden slipway on 26 March 1905, at Issy-les-Moulineaux, near Paris, the glider succeeded only in breaking up in mid-air.

Ferber, who meanwhile had had limited

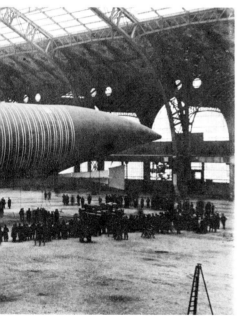

River Seine by a motorboat, and glided for 150 metres (about 500 feet), repeating this flight on 18 June, the same day that Blériot's glider made its maiden flight. The Voisin gliders used a combination of Wright and Hargrave designs, and it was this marriage of the box-kite concept and the Wright formula which was to lay the basis of early European aeroplane flight.

The best that could be managed in England was yet another development of S.F. Cody's man-lifting kites. This was in fact a kite-glider fitted with R.E.P.-type elevons, which was launched from a balloon to glide earthwards.

At the same time, there was real progress being made in Europe with the early dirigible which, by contrast, was being neglected in the United States. While the day of the dirigible was still to come, Santos-Dumont persevered with his small, squashy machines in France, and in Germany, the Count Ferdinand von Zeppelin was testing his already practical airships. The Lebaudy brothers and their airships were still prominent. Their first truly practical airships were favoured by the French military authorities. In October 1905, for example, the Lebaudy 'steerable balloon' visited a number of military installations, practising the discharge of projectiles and aerial photography.

The conventional balloon was enjoying sporting prominence, even to the extent of an inaugural meeting of the Aero Club, later the Royal Aero Club, founded in 1901, being held in a balloon. One founder member, J.T.C. Moore-Brabazon, later Lord Brabazon of Tara, characteristically took a pig with him on one balloon ascent, simply to prove that pigs could fly!

But probably the most significant European contribution to aeronautics at this time was the founding of the Fédération Aéronautique Internationale in Paris in 1905, by the Comte Henri de la Vaulx. During the years to come this became the recognised authority for the ratification of aeronautical records and the control of sporting events involving aircraft. It was a wise move to establish such an institution before the pace of aircraft development quickened, as it was to do – and quite disproportionately – before long.

success with a stable glider design, built a larger version and installed a 12hp Peugeot engine to drive two tractor propellers, which were fitted to the front elevator. This succeeded in making some powered glides when released from an overhead launching cable on 25 May at Chalais-Meudon, but failed to make controlled sustained flight.

Rather more promising for the future of European aviation at this dull period, Gabriel Voisin built two float-gliders for Archdeacon and for Blériot. On 8 June, the Archdeacon model was towed off the

During the early years of the century, the expatriate Brazilian Alberto Santos-Dumont continued his experiments with airships, of which his most famous was the No. 6, shown here, in which he made his epic flight around the Eiffel Tower, in October 1901.

The first practical airship was the Lebaudy No. 1, or 'Jaune' because of its yellow colour, which, after being rebuilt following an accident, remained in service, primarily making demonstration flights, during the early years of the century. It was first completed in 1902.

2
EUROPE TAKES OFF

Santos-Dumont, Cody, Curtiss, Archdeacon, Vuia, Levavasseur, Ellehammer, Farman, Voisin, Ferber, Blériot

'The demonstration that no combination of known forces, known form of machinery, and known forms of force can be united in a practicable machine by which men shall fly seems to the writer as complete as it is possible for the demonstration of any physical fact to be.'
Simon Newcomb
(*1906*)

lberto Santos-Dumont arrived in Paris in 1898. A wealthy young Brazilian, he differed from the typical playboy attracted by the pleasures of a city probably at the zenith of its charms. He used Paris as a stage for his considerable aeronautical exploits. Almost immediately his enthusiasm was fired by the possibilities of flight. Initially he experimented with a series of small, indeed rather squashy airships of which the most famous was the No. VI, the vehicle for his famous journey from St Cloud on 19 October 1901, during the course of which he circled the Eiffel Tower.

His interest in powered heavier-than-air flight may have been accidentally aroused. He visited the St Louis Exposition in 1904, and it was there that he met Octave Chanute, and learnt for himself of the Wright brothers' achievements. This first inspired him to design, build and test a completely unsuccessful helicopter design in 1905, but before long he was testing a most unlikely aeroplane, owing something to the Wrights, to Hargrave, and even to Voisin, in its design. Rather in the manner of Jacob Degen, he first tested this aeroplane by suspending it under his balloon, No. 14, in July 1906 with the appropriate designation, '14-bis'.

Santos-Dumont must have been acutely

First flight in Europe! Alberto Santos-Dumont, a Brazilian living in France, made a number of attempts at flight at Bagatelle, during 1906, using his Antoinette-powered '14' biplane, incorporating Wright and Hargrave features. He was denied success at first, with inadequate power and means of control, but after a 50hp engine was fitted to his machine, with ailerons between the wings, the re-named 14-bis made a hop flight of 220 metres, almost 700 feet, in 21.5 seconds on 12 November 1906.

The 14-bis at its inter-
mediate stage, with
the 50hp engine fitted,
when it managed to
fly for all of 25 metres,
about 80 feet, in
October. No ailerons
at this stage!

disappointed when, at Bagatelle on 13 September 1906, his aeroplane only succeeded in making a few tentative hops before crash-landing. The aerodynamic advantages of having a 'boxed-in' biplane mainplane and foreplane, and the power of a 24hp Antoinette engine to drive a pusher-propeller, proved to be insufficient. The aircraft had also been flight-tested from an overhead trolley wire as an interim stage between balloon-supported tests and the attempt at sustained flight. However, controlled flight from such a machine was too much to hope for – among other essentials, the 14-bis lacked a tailplane.

Undaunted, Santos-Dumont fitted a larger, 50hp, Antoinette engine and on 23 October the 14-bis won an Archdeacon-sponsored prize with a flight of 25 metres. Santos-Dumont next fitted octagonal ailerons between the wings of the mainplane

Just as the Wrights
had their rival, so did
Santos-Dumont in
Europe. The Danish
engineer, Elle-
hammer, made a 42-
metre tethered flight
at Lindholm on 12
September 1906 – he
is seen here with his
wheels just leaving the
ground, possibly after
passing over a bump.
The tethered test
track can be seen
clearly, and the pilot
had no control over
the engine, acting
more as passenger.
Ellehammer's work
formed the basis for
the early attempts
at flight by the
German, Hans Grade.

The engine eventually used by Santos-Dumont, the 50hp Antoinette, which provided a fairly high standard of reliability for its day and was often used by Blériot, although not, it may be said, for his crossing of the English Channel.

and, on 12 November 1906, succeeded in flying 220 metres in 21.5 seconds, winning the Aéro Club de France's prize of 1500 francs (£60) for the first flight of more than 100 metres to be officially observed.

Santos-Dumont's progress may have been little more than a series of hops, but it was eagerly watched, not least by the press:

M. Santos-Dumont not having been able to make his projected attempt to

win the Archeacon–Deutsch prize in September gave formal notice to the Aéro Club and, as the glass was rising, asked the Committee to be at his disposal at 9am. At 10.30am after a first trial in which the motor had failed, he made a second trial. The two wheels of the apparatus once more left the ground and in 5.2 seconds the machine travelled 500 metres, in the course of which it rose four times. Then, as M. Santos-Dumont was trying to effect

A distinctly nautical
air prevails in this
photograph of Léon
Levavasseur, who
master-minded the
rise of the Antoinette
concern during the
first decade of the
century. He was the
firm's chief designer,
and the company
name came from the
proprietor's daughter.

a turn, the machine being at the moment clear of the ground, the motor again failed, with the result that he soon had not sufficient force. The apparatus fell to the ground, damaging the axle of the two wheels which were themselves bent and twisted. The damage being slight, he declared that he could repair it and resume trials at 2pm.

The aeroplane of Blériot and Voisin made but a short hop. The engineer who was clinging to the machine set it going at high speed preparatory to its rising and ran into an obstacle, which it struck with both wheels. The machinery was broken by the shock of the impact . . .'.

This was a report by a London *Times* correspondent of the events of 12 November. In fact Santos-Dumont was not ready until 4.10pm, when he set off with most of the Committee following him in a car, which he soon outpaced! He then managed to make four flights, including the prize-winning one of 220 metres, which reached a speed of some 40kmph and an altitude of just one metre (a little more than three feet)! His prize for this achievement of £60, presented jointly by Ernest Archdeacon and French aviation's other leading patron and benefactor, Henri Deutsch de la Meurthe, was in addition to the prize of just £4 which he received in October for the 25-metre flight!

The Blériot–Voisin machine was a powered development of the 1905 glider, fitted with ailerons and at first a single, and then two 24hp Antoinette motors driving two pusher propellers. Tests on floats on Lake d'Enghien did not result in the aircraft becoming airborne, and the accident recorded by *The Times* at Bagatelle in November was complete and final. It was hardly an auspicious start to what was to become Blériot's brilliant progress in the years before World War I.

Clearly, Santos-Dumont was Europe's leading aeronaut at the time – but in comparison with the Wrights, what an aeronaut! And after all, his homeland was outside Europe – Europe's best was borrowed. Yet, *L'Aérophile* had already published substantial information about the Wright techniques – and this, in turn, was an elaboration of Chanute's talk some three years before. To the frustration of the Committee of the Aéro Club de France, men like Archdeacon persistently refused to believe in the success of the Wrights and spoke of the problems of control as remaining unsolved.

There were other attempts at flight, of course. In August, a Transylvanian, Trajan Vuia, put his No. 1 tractor mono-

It shouldn't have happened this way! A very subdued Robert Esnault-Pelterie in his R.E.P.2 monoplane, at the end of his one-minute, 800-metre flight at Buc on 8 June 1908. This interesting monoplane was his second design.

plane, with a high (and perhaps appropriate) single bat-type wing to the test after several months of frustration and failure. He succeeded in 'flying' a mere 24 metres. The Vuia I has been credited with influencing Blériot in favour of the monoplane but the fact remains that, in further tests lasting until March 1907, the best that could be attained was another hop of just six metres at Issy-les-Moulineaux on 14 October.

A Danish engineer, J.C.H. Ellehammer, was slightly more successful, on 24 September, when he managed to get his Ellehammer II semi-biplane into the air for 42 metres. Some authorities credit Ellehammer with the first European aeroplane flight, but the Ellehammer II was tethered and its pilot was little more than a passenger because he could exercise very little control over his mount. This was a pity, for Ellehammer's weakness in airframe design seems to have been countered by brilliance in powerplant

design and construction.

Fortunately, 1907 was a more successful year for Europe's aviators, or would-be aviators – although this is not to say that there was yet any serious challenge to the Wrights. At least there was less of a tendency to depend entirely upon Wright ideas – the Vuia I providing an example of a trend towards the development of original European ideas in aviation.

In spite of its lack of control in roll, the most promising design of 1907 was that produced early in the year by the Voisin brothers, Gabriel and Charles, for Delagrange. This was another development of the 1905 float-glider, but with a Wright-type mainplane, a forward elevator and a Hargrave box-kite tailplane. At first the elevator was of biplane form and a 50hp Antoinette motor was used to drive a pusher propeller.

The Voisin–Delagrange biplane could not be described as an instant success – it was far more of a milestone along the

The biplane built by Voisin for Henri Farman in September 1907, using the 50hp Antoinette engine. After some tentative early flights, the aircraft was soon setting records and winning prizes, while it also underwent modifications by Farman, who provided a smaller tailplane and replaced the biplane elevator shown here with a monoplane, as well as adding some dihedral to the wings.

The third A.E.A. design, and the first actually by Glenn Curtiss, was the June Bug, which, on 4 July 1908, flew for 5090 feet and won the *Scientific American* prize for the first officially observed flight in the United States. In front of the aircraft, centre of the photograph, is A.M. Herring (an associate of Curtiss), McCurdy, in shirt-sleeves, the Canadian closely associated with the A.E.A., and C.M. Manly, who had attempted to fly the 'Aerodrome A' for Langley.

road to success. Known as the Voisin–Delagrange I, it was taken from the Voisin factory at Billancourt to Bagatelle on 30 March 1907, where it made six short hops with Charles Voisin as pilot. Its best performance on this occasion was a six-second, 60-metre (some 200 feet) flight. A second aircraft was built for another customer, but never flew.

During April, Louis Blériot appeared at Bagatelle with his 'V' monoplane, a one-off design that was unlike any other of Blériot's designs in that it was a tail-first 'canard' with a pusher-propeller. This gave Blériot a total of four hops, the last of just six metres, before crash-landing. Ever optimistic, Blériot then tackled a tandem-wing design, based on the Langley 'Aerodrome A', which was built for him by Louis Peyret and designated the No. VI or 'Libellule' (Dragonfly). This new machine used a 24hp Antoinette engine to drive a single tractor propeller and featured elevons. On 25 July, at Issy-les-Moulineaux, he made a total of eleven hops in the Libellule, the longest consisting of 150 metres (some 500 feet) and 10 seconds.

The first aircraft to fly
in the United States
after the Wrights'
were produced by the
Aerial Experimental
Association, founded
by Dr Graham Bell
and Glenn Curtiss.
This is the A.E.A.'s
first design, the Red
Wing, which flew for
319 feet at Hammonds-
port, New Jersey, on
12 March 1908.

Another photograph
of the June Bug, with
Charles Manly stand-
ing in front of the
camera. The aircraft's
frail structure can be
seen clearly.

In August, however, he crashed the machine during further trials and narrowly escaped serious injury.

Obviously Blériot felt that the No. VI still had possibilities, in spite of its accident and poor performance. It was soon rebuilt in modified form, using a 50hp, 16-cylinder Antoinette engine, and on 17 September, at Issy, he managed a further six hops, the longest of which was for 17 seconds and 184 metres (some 600 feet). The aircraft seems to have been singularly ill-starred, however. An account of events later that day records,

at 4 o'clock this afternoon M. Blériot lifted his aeroplane off the parade ground at Issy-les-Moulineaux. He rose to a height of 15–20 metres when, after he had covered a distance of only 156 metres, the motor suddenly stopped working. The machine descended with great swiftness and was broken to pieces on the ground. M. Blériot picked himself up with his face covered with blood, but without suffering any serious injury.

Having tried to kill himself twice, Blériot was obviously set on making a better job of it next time. He designed and built his No. VII himself, introducing the typical Blériot tractor monoplane, with a two-wheeled undercarriage attached to the wing and a single tailwheel. The tailplane incorporated a rudder and elevons, and the whole design was built to be inherently unstable. It was powered by another 50hp Antoinette motor. Starting on 16 November, at Issy, he managed six short flights in the new machine, of which the two best were for 45 seconds and 500 metres each, and during which he also attempted some very basic turning movements. Alas, on the last flight, in December, Blériot crashed this machine

'Nulli Secundus II', in fact the original rebuilt after the accident. The first British Army airship, the 'Nulli Secundus' used a 50hp Antoinette engine, borrowed by Cody for his British Army Aeroplane No. 1.

The first British airship, the 'Nulli Secundus' in 1907, before it was wrecked in a gale later that year.

too, although he again survived. He abandoned the 'VII'.

Blériot was not alone in his attempts to advance the cause of European aviation. The English pioneer, Horatio Phillips (1845–1924), built a manned and full-sized development of his multiplane test rig of 1894, which he tested during the early summer of 1907 at Streatham. This had four large aerofoil frames mounted in tandem and was powered by a single 20hp engine driving a tractor propeller. It was on this device that Phillips managed to make a 500-foot powered hop before retiring from the aviation scene completely – and perhaps not a little sadly for one who had done much to advance the art of wing design.

Trajan Vuia made a further attempt at flight with his Vuia II, but the best he could achieve with the new machine was a 20-metre hop on 5 July 1907, at Bagatelle.

Delagrange, and his partners, the Voisin brothers, spent the summer months working on the Voisin–Delagrange I. After trials on floats at Lake d'Enghien, the Voisin–Delagrange was refitted with wheels and on 5 November, at Issy-les-Moulineaux, it made two flights, one of which lasted for 500 metres and 40 seconds.

In fact, a third Voisin machine had been built in the meantime for the English-born, French-naturalised Henri Farman (1874–1958). The son of the Paris correspondent of the *Tribune*, Henri Farman was a water-colour artist bitten by the motor-racing bug, from which it was a short step to the infant aeroplane. Sometimes in collaboration, sometimes in friendly competition with his brother Maurice, Henri Farman was to be, in common with Blériot, one of the greatest driving forces in early European aviation. As in the case of Blériot, his early inspiration was the Voisin aeroplane.

The Voisin–Farman I retained the biplane layout of the basic Voisin aeroplane and the same 50hp Antoinette engine. After a tentative first flight in September, the aircraft was able to win the Archdeacon Cup on 26 October for a flight of 771 metres in 52.6 seconds. On 9 November it performed the first European flight of more than a thousand metres by flying 1030 metres in 1 minute

Although completed during spring, 1908, Cody's British Army Aeroplane No. 1 could not be flown until the following year, for want of a powerplant, which was eventually borrowed from the airship 'Nulli Secundus'. It is shown here being man-handled in preparation for the first flight.

Engine in place and obviously working! Cody's British Army Aeroplane No. 1, showing its close relationship to the Wrights' concepts. Before this, Cody had experimented by fitting an engine to one of his large kites.

14 seconds – the longest European flight at that time and also the first to last longer than one minute. Farman made a few modifications to the aircraft, as if to establish some claim to a share in its development. He replaced the box-kite tailplane with a smaller tailplane of similar layout, converted the elevator from biplane to monoplane configuration, and added some dihedral to the wings.

Esnault-Pelterie followed the example of his fellow-countryman, Louis Blériot, in concentrating on the monoplane, starting in 1907 with the R.E.P. 1, which had bird-form wings and a 25hp engine. This eventually managed to make five hops at Buc in November and December 1907, the best of which was for 600 metres or 55 seconds on 16 November. Some primitive means of control in roll was applied to the R.E.P. 1, although Esnault-Pelterie still could not grasp the principles on which Wilbur and Orville Wright had worked. Another monoplane was designed by Victor Tatin and De la Vaulx. It had a 50hp Antoinette engine driving two pusher propellers. This machine was built by Mallet and made two tentative hops at St Cyr on 18 November before crashing.

Another French pioneer, De Pischof,

The first real British aeroplane, Alliott Verdon Roe's Roe I biplane, which managed to make a 150-foot hop at Brooklands in June 1908, but had to be towed downhill by a car to achieve even this!

built a biplane with a 25hp Anzani engine driving a single tractor propeller. Put to the test at Issy on 6 December, the best that it could achieve was a hop of just seven metres! Further trials on 15 June 1908 resulted in a seven-second flight of 84 metres.

Ellehammer was still hard at work at Lindholm, building his Ellehammer III triplane, again with an engine of his own design. This made a few miserable hops during the winter of 1907–8.

In England, Cody, at Farnborough, fitted a 12hp Buchet motor to a man-carrying kite of his own design, and flew it, unmanned, as a 'powered kite'. His was only the visible indication of official British interest in aircraft, for J.W. Dunne was working in secret at Blair Atholl in Scotland on a swept-wing biplane. This was tested first as a glider and then with two 12hp Buchet motors, but the project disappointed by crashing on take-off.

Not all gliders were immediately seen

as protypes for powered aircraft, but perhaps one of the most promising, longer-term developments of this nature came from the testing of a swept-wing mono-plane glider, without a tail, at Oberalstadt in Bohemia by I. Etrich and F. Wels. This was the predecessor of the famous Rumpler–Etrich Taube monoplane of 1910.

The development of the dirigible was progressing well. There were some notable flights at this time, including one of $4\frac{1}{2}$ hours by a Zeppelin on 24 September, and another of 3 hours on the following day. In each case there were at least nine passengers in the car. Balloons, too, were still making news, with what one newspaper described as an 'impromptu race to the coast'. This took place on Sunday, 10 November, between three balloons; the 'Valkyrie' with the Honourable Charles Rolls, of Rolls-Royce fame, in command, the 'Satellite' and the 'Royal Aero Club No. 2'. All three ascended from Short Brothers' balloon works near Chelsea in London, and the race ended on the English Channel coast near Seaford, in a thick mist with the balloons descending to the sound of ships' whistles. The Valkyrie won.

It was at this time that the United States War Department decided that it really ought to have a dirigible, and commissioned the design and construction of one for \$25,000 (£5000).

Perhaps a little off the mainstream of aeronautical development at the time, the Breguet brothers and Richet had built the first full-sized helicopter test-rig at Douai. On 29 September, this actually succeeded in making a tentative man-carrying tethered flight, powered by a 50hp Antoinette motor. This was followed on 13 November, by the Paul Cornu helicopter, powered by a 24hp Antoinette motor which drove two laterally-offset rotorblades; this succeeded in making a tentative man-carrying flight at Lisieux. Neither machine could be considered to be practical, but the Cornu flight at least was untethered.

During this period the Wright brothers had been quietly negotiating, building up their contacts in both Europe and the United States. They had also designed an improved Flyer III – today generally referred to as the 'Wright A biplane' –

which used a 30hp Wright engine. The brothers had also realised how little they had to fear from European competition so, when the Wright A arrived in France at Le Havre towards the end of 1907, they were content for it to winter in store.

The pace of aeroplane development quickened in 1908 on both sides of the Atlantic. It was almost as if the rivals of the Wrights must have realised that the brothers were about to reappear on the aviation scene. European efforts to catch-up with the Wrights were soon to be seen to be fruitless but, in the meantime, there was a lot of flying to be done. The self-opinionated Europeans were soon to suffer the bitter truth about themselves!

Farman started to fly his modified Voisin–Farman '1-bis' at Issy on 11 January, preparing for an attempt on the prize of 50,000 francs (£2000) offered jointly

by Ernest Archdeacon and Henri Deutsch de La Meurthe. The prize, the 'Grand Prix d'Aviation', was offered for the first powered, heavier-than-air machine to fly over a circular course, although this in reality was purely a European event. Success came to Farman on 13 January, according to *The Times:*

In the domain of the air, the number 13 would appear by all events to bring good luck. This morning, a little after 10am, Mr. Henri Farman, succeeded in rising in a machine of his own invention, flying a kilometre to a goal previously fixed, which he rounded in perfect conditions of stability, and in returning to his starting point where he succeeded in alighting without a hitch. Nothing of the kind has ever before been accomplished. Mr. Farman thus

won the 50,000 francs (£2,000) prize offered by M. Henry Deutsch and M. Archdeacon.

This was a flight of 1500 metres taking 1 minute 28 seconds. Reporters described the aircraft as being related to the Chanute two-surface gliding machine, now well known in Europe, and as having a wing area of 52 square metres and an airframe 10 metres in length. Henri Farman was the guest of honour at an Aéro Club de France banquet. No doubt full of himself, Farman was to modify the airframe of his machine and to substitute a 50hp Renault engine for the Antoinette, re-naming the aircraft as the Henri Farman I, although he later reverted to the original powerplant.

Delagrange did not let such flying pass unchallenged, buying another aircraft

Santos-Dumont enjoyed only slight success with his No. 19 Demoiselle, an ultra-light aeroplane which first appeared in November 1907.

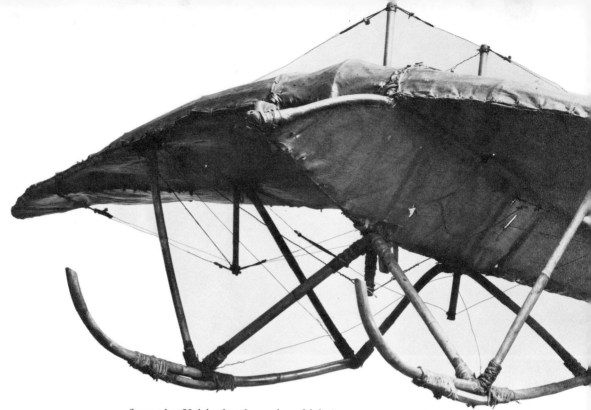

from the Voisin brothers, in which he flew for 3925 metres, taking six-and-a-half minutes, at Issy on 11 April 1908. Subsequently modified to a semi-Hargrave style, the aircraft was re-designated the Voisin–Delagrange III, and flew for 14.27 kilometres in $18\frac{1}{2}$ minutes in a demonstration flight at Milan on 23 June. Delagrange went on to make the first passenger-carrying flight with a woman, Madame Thérèse Peltier, on 8 July, at Turin. Madame Peltier in fact became the first woman to fly an aeroplane, although she never qualified for a pilot's certificate. The first passenger flight had already been made in the United States by Orville Wright on a modified Wright Flyer III, when C.W. Furnas was taken up, on 14 May, at the Kill Devil Hills, for a flight of $2\frac{1}{2}$ miles and 3 minutes 40 seconds. The first European passenger-carrying flight took place on 29 May, when Henri Farman took up Ernest Archdeacon.

Among the other early French aviators, Ferber and Esnault-Pelterie both returned to the fray in early 1908, although Ferber soon amalgamated his energies into the Antoinette concern, becoming a maker of airframes as well as engines. Disappointingly, Esnault-Pelterie's R.E.P. 2 monoplane denied him the success which

he still craved, attaining just 800 metres and 1 minute at Buc on 8 June.

At this time the Antoinette concern was falling short of the considerable success it was to achieve at a later date. The firm's proprietor, Gastambide, was building the Gastambide–Mengin I design, the brainchild of his chief designer, Léon Levavasseur, which only succeeded in flying for 150 metres at Bagatelle on 13 February. The name, Antoinette, incidentally, came from the proprietor's young daughter.

Most surprising of all, perhaps, it was only at this comparatively late date that American competition for the Wright brothers emerged – for one can safely discount the enterprising Cody's exploits on behalf of the British Army. The spread of interest in flight in the United States coincided with the founding of the Aerial Experimental Association, by Dr Graham Bell and Glenn Curtiss at Hammondsport, New Jersey. This also signified the start of Curtiss's interest in aviation – by slight coincidence, he was a motor-cycle manufacturer.

The first A.E.A. design was the work of the unfortunate Lieutenant Selfridge. This was the 'Red Wing', flown for 319 feet at Hammondsport on 12 March 1908.

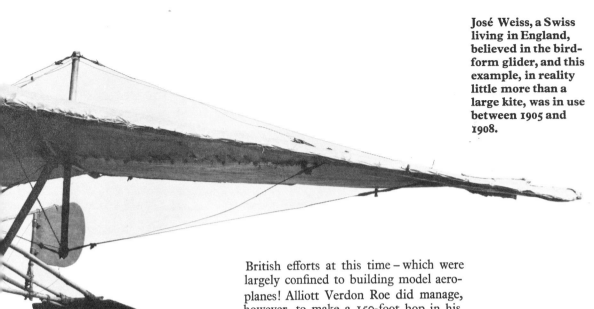

It resembled the Wright aircraft in some respects: it had a biplane mainplane, a monoplane elevator foreplane, and a biplane tailplane, with ailerons for control in roll. This machine was soon followed by 'White Wing', the work of Red Wing's pilot, F.W. Baldwin, which closely resembled the earlier aircraft, and was flown by Glenn Curtiss for five flights on 21 May, the longest of which lasted for 1017 feet and 19 seconds. Curtiss's own first aircraft design was the 'June Bug'. It first flew in June 1908, and went on to win the *Scientific American* trophy for the first officially-observed flight in the United States. The best of its 54 flights came on 4 July, and covered 5090 feet in 1 minute 42½ seconds. The start of a long and protracted fight between the Wright brothers and Curtiss came at this time, for Orville, learning that Curtiss was using ailerons on his June Bug, wrote to him in July 1908, alleging infringement of the Wright brothers' wing-warping patents.

Before the end of the year, in December, Curtiss and the A.E.A. attempted to fly a hydro-aeroplane, the 'Loon', but without success. Meanwhile, ever hopeful, the Ellehammer No. IV made a number of flights at Kiel in Germany, but the longest of these was only for 400 metres in 11 seconds, on 28 June.

An atmosphere of farce surrounded the British efforts at this time – which were largely confined to building model aeroplanes! Alliott Verdon Roe did manage, however, to make a 150-foot hop in his Roe I biplane at Brooklands in June 1908, but only while being towed by a car or after a downhill run! S.F. Cody, however, completed his British Army Aeroplane No. I, with Colonel Capper's assistance, at Farnborough during the spring. Flight trials of this aeroplane could not be started, however, because the engine, a 50hp Antoinette, was being used on the British Army's first airship, the 'Nulli Secundus', also undergoing trials at the time! Basically, the British Army Aeroplane No. I was an aircraft of the Wright type, with biplane mainplane, a forward elevator and a rear rudder. Balloons and airships were very much to the fore in British military thinking at this time. Successful ground-to-air wireless transmissions had been made to the aerostat Pegasus over a distance of 20 miles.

Louis Blériot, meanwhile, had completed his No. VIII monoplane, powered by a 50hp Antoinette engine. He was able to fly it for the first time at Issy on 29 June, for just 50 seconds over a distance of 700 metres. This aircraft differed from his earlier models by incorporating wing-tip ailerons mounted on pivots. After modification, as the VIII-bis, it flew for 8 minutes 25 seconds on 6 July. The Blériot VIII has generally been regarded as the first typical Blériot.

The first half of 1908 had seen Europe's best efforts to date in the field of aviation. But the Europeans were now to see just how far behind America they really were!

3
A SOCIAL OCCASION

Wilbur's début, passenger-carrying flights, accidents, Antoinette, Blériot, Farman, Cody, Moore-Brabazon, across the Channel, the dirigible threat

'The machine at present shows its superiority over our aeroplanes, but have patience! In a little while, Mr Wright will be equalled and even surpassed.'
Louis Blériot
(*1908*)

The small local racecourse at Hunaudières, five miles south of the now famous Le Mans, was the setting for one of the milestones in aeronautical history. On 8 August 1908, at 6.30pm, Wilbur Wright took off in his Wright A biplane. He flew for just 1 minute and 45 seconds, but his flight demonstrated such complete mastery of the air that his critical audience, drawn from the French aviation establishment, was immediately convinced, not only of American supremacy in the air, but of the complete authenticity of the Wright claims.

Perhaps the event and the emotions it generated were best described by the French newspaper, *Le Figaro*, which gave its readers a resumé of events:

It is not the first time that a man has risen from the earth in a machine heavier than air, but yesterday's achievement re-establishes the historical truth and repairs an injustice. Hitherto, the honour of the first flight had been attributed to M. Santos-Dumont, whose merits remain what they have always been. That attempt took place on September 10, 1906, on the lawn of Bagatelle in Paris. Now the first flight of the Wright Brothers took place in 1901. They were renewed and perfected during the four succeeding years, and, although guaranteed by a witness whose competency ought to have been sufficient authority for the statement, namely Mr Octave Chanute, the Chicago professor who is an expert in aviation, nothing but incredulity reigned in Europe, and even in America. The Messrs Wright were called humbugs and regarded as 'bluffers', the more so as they followed up their experiments with negotiations for the sale at high prices in the old and

FLIGHT

A Journal devoted to the Interests, Practice, and Progress of
——— Aerial Locomotion and Transport. ———

No. 1.   NOVEMBER 5, 1908.   PRICE ONE PENNY.

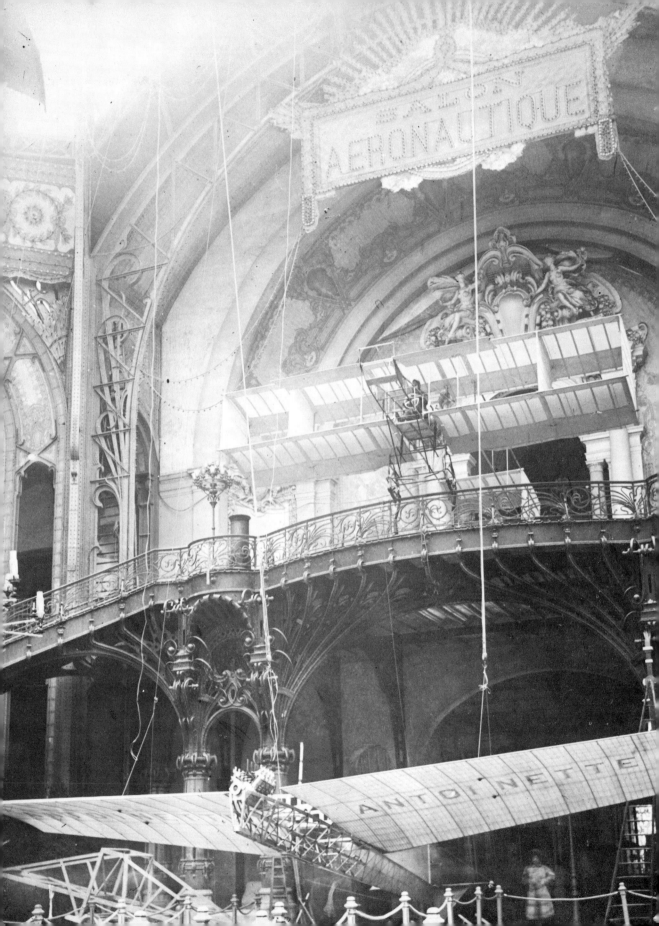

the new world of the patents of their machine. In 1905, pourparlers were begun by France for the purchase of the Wright aeroplane. They resulted, in 1906, in an option to MM. Fordyce, Henri Letellier and Desouches, who suddenly felt doubts and ceded their options to the American Government. Thereupon the French Government intervened and, on the urgent advice of Captain Ferber, decided to act. M. Etienne, then Minister for War, sent a mission to the United States. He offered the Wright Brothers 600,000 francs (£24,000) for their machine on condition that they should previously execute a flight of 50 kilometres at an altitude of 300 metres.

This condition put an end to the negotiations. But in April, 1908, M. Lazare Weiller, the well-known manufacturer, entered into pourparlers with the Wright brothers and signed a contract with them according to which he became for 500,000 francs (£20,000) the proprietor of the aeroplane if, before the end of 1908, their machine, with two persons on board, accomplished a flight of 50 kilometres. Yesterday's trial showed that the Wright aeroplane will fulfil the stipulated condition ... it had on board ... a burden representative of the second person in the form of a heavy sack.

Wilbur Wright himself had told a reporter: 'When in the air, I made no fewer than ten mistakes, due to the fact that I had been laying off so long, but I corrected them all rapidly so I do not suppose that any one watching really knew that I made mistakes at all. I was much pleased with the way in which my first trial in France was received.'

So he should have been! Blériot was one of those watching:

I consider that, for us in France and elsewhere, a new era in mechanical flight has begun. I am not sufficiently calm after the event thoroughly to express my opinions. My view can but be described in the words – It is marvellous ... The machine at present shows its superiority over our aeroplanes, but have patience! In a little while, Mr Wright will be equalled and even surpassed.

The Wright A was a modified Flyer III with a 30hp Wright engine. In April 1908, Wilbur and Orville had returned to the Kill Devil Hills with a 'III', modified to take two persons sitting upright, and gave themselves what was, in effect, a refresher course in flying. On 14 May, the two brothers took it in turn to give C.W. Furnas the first passenger flights in an aeroplane. Meanwhile, the first 'A' had remained in store at Le Havre, where Wilbur arrived at the end of May. He readily accepted Léon Bollée's suggestion

The Paris Aero Salon of 1908 saw both the new Antoinette monoplane, developed from the Gastambide-Mengin of earlier that same year, and the Farman-Voisin I on display.

Success eventually came to Santos-Dumont's Demoiselle in November 1908, by which time it not only had a new engine, but the engine position was moved to between the wheels. An idea of its small size can be gained from this photograph of the Demoiselle in transit.

49

that he should re-assemble the aircraft at his factory at Le Mans. After some difficulty in obtaining replacement items for those parts of the aircraft damaged in store and in transit, he was ready to fly again in August and had sufficient confidence in himself and in his machine not to require secret practice flights.

Such was the change in French attitudes that, from this time on, Wilbur was followed everywhere by a group of admiring enthusiasts and his every movement was widely reported. To be fair, he did not revel in the glory he had created for himself, being an exceptionally modest and withdrawn man by nature.

After completing nine flights at Hunaudières, Wilbur was granted permission to use the Camp d'Auvours, a large military training ground seven miles east of Le Mans. It was here that he was to complete one hundred flights by the end of December. It was here, too, on a day when flying was suspended by Wilbur, and by the Europeans at Issy-les-Moulineaux due to bad weather, that the Baron d'Estournelles de Constant presented medals to Wilbur for himself and his brother.

The year 1908 saw a succession of magnificent achievements from the Wright A. On 21 September, it set an endurance record of 91 minutes, covering $41\frac{1}{3}$ miles, and on 3 October, a 55-minute passenger-carrying flight covered $34\frac{3}{4}$ miles. These were, respectively, the first flight of more

The French government airship, 'République' of 1908, still followed the basic Lebaudy design.

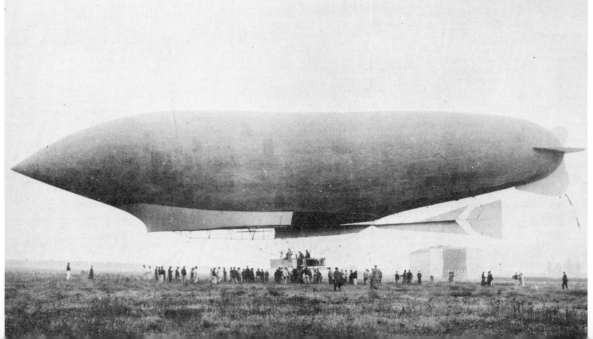

than 90 minutes and the first passenger flight of more than 30 minutes. Wilbur also made the first passenger flight of more than an hour on 10 October, which lasted for almost 70 minutes and covered 50 miles. He went on to end a successful year with a solo flight of 140 minutes on 31 December, covering 78 miles and winning the Michelin Trophy of 20,000 francs (£800).

Not that the French were standing still meanwhile. The modified Voisin–Delagrange III biplane made the first European flight of more than half-an-hour on 17 September at Issy. Farman made a flight of 40 kilometres at the Camp de Chalons on 2 October and then, on 30 October, made the first cross-country flight, flying from Bouy to Reims, a distance of 27 kilometres, in 20 minutes.

He used the modified Voisin–Farman I-bis for this flight. On the following day he set an official altitude record of 80 feet with the same machine. In fact he had been photographed flying over some 90-foot poplar trees with ease between Bouy and Reims.

Both of the Voisin machines had had their mainplanes modified to incorporate additional side curtains to give the maximum 'box-kite' effect, and the Farman had four large flap-type ailerons. The Farman was also later to undergo a temporary transformation to a near-triplane layout.

The first true Antoinette was evolved from the Gastambide–Mengin I of early 1908, and the work of Ferber and Levavasseur; flap-type ailerons on the IV and V were also employed on the

Unsuccessful and frequently overlooked, the A.E.A. 'Loon' of December 1908, was an early attempt to build a 'water aeroplane', and provided Curtiss with an opportunity to try his hand at hydro-aeroplane design.

Antoinette. However, the other major monoplane proponent, Blériot, used pivoting wing-tip ailerons on his VIII-bis. The Blériot VIII-bis flew the return Touray–Artenay flight on 31 October, a distance of 28 kilometres, which would have been more significant were it not for two landings en route. At the same time, Alberto Santos-Dumont was still having difficulties with his diminutive Demoiselle ultra-light monoplane, in which the pilot sat inside the bamboo framework of the fuselage. Esnault-Pelterie's R.E.P. 2 and R.E.P. 2-bis, the latter using Wright-type wing-warping, were not completely successful either.

Neither of two triplane designs, the Goupy tractor triplane and the De Caters, built by the Voisins, were successful, and the Koechlin-de Pischoff monoplane only succeeded in flying for 40 seconds over a distance of 500 metres at Villacoubly in October.

Relatively little success, too, attended the flights of the British Army Aeroplane No. 1, built by S.F. Cody at Farnborough, although this was now able to use the Antoinette engine salvaged from the wrecked 'Nulli Secundus' airship. Test flights with Cody as pilot started on 19

A close-up of the nacelle of the 'République', showing its rudimentary construction.

Louis Blériot saw that 1909 got off to a flying start, with his cross-country flights on the Blériot II.

September, but the best flight, one of 1390 feet on 16 October, ended with a crash landing. The British could take some comfort from the fact that the balloonist, J.T.C. Moore-Brabazon, became the first Briton (Cody was still officially an American citizen) to qualify as a pilot.

If the achievements of the Wright brothers are discounted, the Americans were not doing particularly well at this time themselves. The A.E.A.'s newest biplane, the Silver Dart, flew for a minute-and-a-half and covered 5280 feet at Hammondsport on 17 December, in the hands of its designer, the Canadian, Douglas McCurdy.

Orville Wright had in fact been busy in the United States at Fort Myer, putting a new Wright A through its paces in a series of ten flights starting on 3 September. Four of these lasted for longer than an hour, and Orville was also able to add unofficial altitude records of 200 and 310 feet to his achievements. His first flight over the hour was on 9 September, and took $62\frac{1}{4}$ minutes. This time was not to be bettered by a European until a pupil of Wilbur Wright's, Paul Tissandier, flew for 62 minutes in early 1909. Meanwhile, the younger brother also managed to collect some prize money, totalling $35,000 (£7000), for his efforts.

Rivals to the Wright brothers sprang up. Augustus Moore-Herring asked to be considered against Orville Wright in the

United States War Department trials, optimistically promising the high speed of 80mph from a new and, as then, unfinished design. A little later, Thomas Edison recorded his opinion that eventually the helicoptal aeroplane would be able to take-off vertically and safely, although he conceded that this was not practical as yet!

Two witnesses of Orville's achievements at Fort Myer were the head of the British Army's Balloon Section, Colonel J.L.B. Templer, and his American counterpart, Major George Squier, U.S.

Army. Both spoke highly of the aircraft, Templer saying: 'Mr Wright could fly to New York, a distance of 250 miles, now, if he wanted to. It is the most wonderful flying machine in the world. Success was assured from the start. I have always believed in the Wrights and in what they would do.' According to Squier, the U.S. War Department's doubts were clearly gone, for: 'It is the best sport I know of. It is a magnificent sensation flying without a gasbag. I will have a regular aeronautical station at Fort Myer from now on.'

Unfortunately, disaster was just around the corner amidst such high hopes and higher praise. On 17 September, flying with Lieutenant Selfridge as passenger, a young signals officer and designer of the first A.E.A. aircraft, one of the two new propellers on the aircraft shattered. Control was immediately lost and the aircraft fell to the ground 'with a sickening thud'. An eyewitness reported:

I happened to be among the first to come on the scene of the disaster and I found the aeroplane crumpled up

Blériot is best remembered for this, the first aeroplane flight across the English Channel, early in the morning of 25 July 1909.

Hubert Latham, flying his Antoinette under happier, and dryer, conditions.

The attractive poster for the Reims Aviation Week, August 1909.

and the passengers lying motionless amongst the splintered framework. Lieutenant Selfridge, in particular, was bleeding profusely from the head, and when removed both he and Mr Wright were still unconscious.

A few hours later, poor Selfridge was dead. Wilbur, on hearing the news, immediately withdrew from a flying contest, filled with remorse for the fate of Selfridge and concern over the fate of his brother.

Not all of the aeronautical events of the year were concerned with the aeroplane, although it was clearly stealing the limelight. Count Ferdinand von Zeppelin had been receiving a fairly brisk flow of orders from various governments for his dirigibles. There were frequent reports of plans for dirigible air services on both sides of the Atlantic. The Count announced that he had formed his firm into a limited liability company on 21 September. Germany was clearly doing her best to compensate for her lack of success with the aeroplane. On Saturday, 10 November, twenty-five balloons took part in an International Balloon Race, organised by

the Berlin Aero Club, with no less than seventeen of the entries from Germany, six from Belgium, and one each from France and Austria. There were twenty-two entries for the Gordon–Bennett Balloon Contest, also held that year at Berlin on the day after the International Race. This saw a near disaster to an American balloon, 'Conqueror', which was damaged on take-off and crashed, happily without injury to its occupants, two miles further on.

There was a sinister side to the German enthusiasm for aerostation – French public opinion was alarmed at the number of German balloons, and dirigibles, which strayed over and often force-landed on the French side of the frontier, often while carrying army personnel. Even at this time, espionage was suspected, and the Germans were felt to be studying French defences.

The year 1909 promised even greater things for the aeroplane, although this was also a year in which the Imperial German Navy had four Zeppelin airships on order, and the Russians ordered a Lebaudy airship, identical to 'La République', then under construction for the French Army. And, at long last, the United States Senate awoke to events and decided that the Secretary of State for War should award gold medals to the Wright brothers for their achievements.

200.000F. de PRIX
GRANDE
SEMAINE
E. Montaut
D'AVIATION DE LA
REIMS DU 22 AU 29 AOÛT 1909 CHAMPAGNE

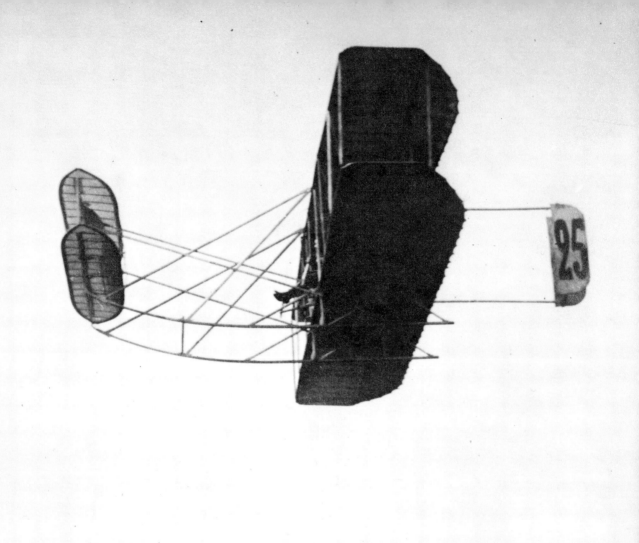

Opposite:
One of the more notable of the Reims aviators was Eugene Lefebvre, who established an unofficial record in his Wright A; shown here flying past the grandstands.

Low speeds meant that there was little need for specialised flying clothes – hence the almost everyday attire of Lefebvre, sitting in his Wright A.

Wilbur Wright had by this time established a flying school at Pau, in the South of France. British and French firms, including Short Brothers and Bollée, started to build the Wright A under licence, too. A total of seven aircraft of this type were also built by the brothers themselves, some with dual-controls for training. Wilbur Wright even had an English pupil at Pau, Hubert Latham. He was soon to make a name for himself as an enterprising pilot and as the first man to roll and light a cigarette while flying an aeroplane! Many of Latham's achievements were to take place while flying Antoinette monoplanes. In the meantime, another of Wilbur's pupils, Paul Tissandier, flew a Wright A for $35\frac{3}{4}$ miles, in just 62 minutes, so becoming not only the first European to fly for more than an hour, but also establishing the first official speed record of 34.04mph. This was on 20 May.

Much of the interest of the year was to centre around the first aviation meeting to be recognised as such, at Reims in late

British journal, *Flight*. This had been formed as a supplement to the *Automotor* in late 1908, and had had a separate existence from the beginning of 1909 as the first aeronautical weekly in the world and the official organ of the Aero Club. A German Aerostation Company had been formed, with plans for passenger and freight services between thirty depots throughout the German Empire. In the United States a mail and passenger service was planned to link New York and Boston.

The French unfortunately managed to lose their dirigible 'La Patrie', which was blown from its moorings during a high wind and was last seen over Ireland, where its progress was delayed slightly by

Latham flying over Lefebvre's machine at Reims.

August. But before this an aviation meeting of a kind got underway at Monaco. It lasted from Sunday, 24 January to 24 March, but no one turned up at first, so the meeting was extended until 24 April. The interest abroad in aviation meetings and in establishing flying fields prompted the British pioneer, N. Pemberton-Billing, to buy land at Farnbridge, between the Thames and the Crouch, where he founded what was in effect a flying field with club facilities for British pilots. The need for this is not clear, since The Aero Club already had an airfield and sheds at Eastchurch, on the Isle of Sheppey.

Cody, meanwhile, had got his British Army Aeroplane No. I flying again and was giving demonstration flights at Laffan's Plain, Farnborough.

Continued interest in airships, and the announcement of more plans for airship services, were ridiculed by the new

a collision with a hilltop! The French Army thus had to wait for the new 'La République' to be completed. Rather than see his country thus deprived, the patriotic Henri Deutsch de la Meurthe gave them his own 'La Ville de Paris'.

French doubts about German intentions with regard to airships were becoming more severe. The Zeppelin No. I made a flight on 19 March carrying seven Army officers, three N.C.O.s, and fifteen soldiers in addition to the crew. It flew for four hours, covering 150 miles at an altitude of up to 650 feet. This event also prompted fears in Britain about what might happen should such an airship hover over the vaults of the Bank of England with a bomb!

Early in 1909, Wilbur Wright was joined in France by Orville, now fully recovered, and by their sister, Katherine, who frequently accompanied Orville after his accident. Although taken up as a passenger on a number of occasions, Katherine declined to learn to fly – but it was noted that she made rather better progress in learning French than either of her brothers!

In 1909, Blériot's boast that the French would surpass the achievements of the Wrights began to look like a possibility. The weak power units of the early aircraft gave way to a new breed of improved engines, many of which were from France. Apart from an improved Antoinette, they included the Anzani and

Much of the success of Reims lay in its ability to attract major public and political figures – here is the then President of France, Fallières.

the rotary Gnome, both air-cooled and the latter being a development of a basic Hargrave concept, which substituted internal combustion for compressed air, and the water-cooled Vivinus. In air-frame development, too, the French were now pushing ahead, with the Goupy II and Breguet I tractor biplanes setting the pattern for the planes of World War I and after. The Blériot XI monoplane and the Antoinette VI and VII mono-planes used wing-warping, while Henri Farman used ailerons on his Vivinus-powered Farman III. It was at this time that the other Farman brother, Maurice, started to take an interest in aviation, although he based his work on the now-dated Voisin design and enjoyed little success at first. Even the Wright's cus-tomers were fitting wheels to their air-craft to replace the skids and launching apparatus.

In March, about a month before the appearance of the Farman III, Santos-Dumont introduced his No. 20, the up-dated and much improved Demoiselle monoplane, with a three-pole bamboo fuselage. The Demoiselle was soon flying successfully and was ready to enter limited production in 1910.

First flights were being made in a number of countries. Hans Grade was the first German to fly an aeroplane when he took off in his development of Ellehammer's design. He also built and flew a monoplane similar to the Demoiselle

One of the oddities of Reims was this, the first Breguet biplane.

Glenn Curtiss in his 'Golden Flier' or 'Reims Machine', which flew well, only just failing to win the Gordon-Bennett Cup; earlier in the day, he had set a record of 43 mph.

late in the year. The German tradition of sailplane flying was revived by Weiss, with his swept-wing, bird-form design.

Curtiss, in the United States, had built his 'Golden Flier', a development of the earlier June Bug. This incorporated ailerons and a fixed tricycle undercarriage, although it still possessed a forward elevator and a tailplane. With the 'Golden Flier', Curtiss, still locked in legal battle with the Wrights, was in a position to challenge the brothers' lead in aeroplane development.

Esnault-Pelterie and the Voisin brothers were slowly falling behind all these new advances, failing to keep pace with developments. The Wrights themselves were no longer in the forefront of their field.

The first big event of the year occurred when a London newspaper, the *Daily Mail*, offered a £1000 prize for the first pilot to fly across the English Channel. The dashing Anglo-French pilot, Hubert Latham, made the first attempt, taking off from Sangatte, near Calais, at 6.42am on Monday, 19 July, in an Antoinette IV. He suffered engine failure while only seven or eight miles out and was forced to ditch, not for the last time. Louis Blériot took off from Les Baraques, near Calais, in his No. XI at 4.40am on the following Sunday and landed, with the minimum of fuss, near Dover Castle at 5.20am, in time for a very early breakfast! Latham, determined at least to be the first Englishman to cross the Channel, took off again on 27 July, at 5.30am from Cap Blanc Nez, in an Antoinette VI with the new sixteen-cylinder 100hp engine. This time he succeeded in nearing the English Coast before being forced to ditch the machine again with engine failure. Interestingly, Blériot had swapped his usual Antoinette engine for an Anzani for the Channel flight.

The Comte de Lambert, Wilbur's first pupil, had planned to fly across the Channel, as had Wilbur himself, but Blériot's apparently effortless success made the exercise rather pointless! Blériot seemed to be leading a charmed existence, but Madame Blériot, with five little Blériots to think about, apparently insisted that her husband stop flying after the Reims meeting – although she later relented.

Reims Week was a major event for the

Curtiss in his 'Reims Machine' – note the steering wheel and radiator!

65

aviators. Held on the Plain of Bethany, just outside the ancient city, from 22 to 29 August, the event was sponsored by the champagne industry and was known officially as 'La Grande Semaine d'Aviation de Champagne'. It is impossible to over-estimate the significance of the meeting, for not only was it here that the first important records for speed, altitude and endurance were set, but it was here, too, that the new phenomenon of aviation was brought to the notice of the people – and the governments – of Europe. The champagne industry as the patron of the new art offered prize money to the total of 200,000 francs – sufficient inducement to bring no less than thirty-eight aircraft to the meeting, of which twenty-three actually took part.

Only the weather was disappointing – the programme suffered frequent interruptions because of high winds, but fortunately the few accidents that occurred did not result in any fatalities. All in all, the one hundred and twenty take-offs resulted in eighty-four flights of more than three miles duration. Perhaps the best pointer to the future to emerge from the event was the award of the Grand Prix to Henri Farman. This was for a flight of 180 kilometres in 3 hours 5 minutes in his Farman III. Latham in fact challenged this award on the grounds that Farman had changed the aircraft's standard Vivinus water-cooled engine for an air-cooled Gnome rotary, but it

Few aviators escaped accidents; this is Blériot's XII after a crash, followed by fire.

The real star of Reims was Blériot, who 'flew grandly' in this, his Blériot XII, to win the Gordon-Bennett Cup, at a speed of almost 48mph.

The U.S. Army's first aircraft–a Wright B delivered in 1909. Here it is at Fort Myer, with the Wright launching apparatus, and the weight in the down position.

Inset:
Although the Wrights did not hurry to fit their aircraft with wheels, their customers did not hesitate to do so–this is the U.S. Army Wright B again.

The first Wright
licensees were the
British Short brothers
and the Frenchman,
Léon Bollée. This
photograph shows a
meeting of the Shorts
and the Wrights, at
Mussel Manor, at
Eastchurch on the Isle
of Sheppey, in 1909.
Standing, second from
the left, is Oswald
Short, followed by
brothers Horace and
Eustace; seated are J.
T. C. Moore-Brabazon
(a founder-member of
the Royal Aero Club,
and later Lord Braba-
zon of Tara), Wilbur
and Orville Wright,
and the Honourable
C. S. Rolls, pioneer
pilot, motorist and co-
founder of Rolls-
Royce.

is generally believed that Levavasseur prompted Latham in this action. Later, on 27 August, Farman made the first flight with two passengers, flying 6 miles in 10 minutes.

The first of many speed records from Reims was set by Glenn Curtiss on 23 August. Flying an aircraft identical to his 'Golden Flier', sometimes known as his 'Reims machine', he reached a record of 43.35mph on a windy day on which flying was delayed until 5pm. A casualty was Latham's Antoinette which, according to *The Times*, 'took a header, striking the ground with such violence that the propeller was bent and the machine itself otherwise damaged.' Lefebvre had set up an unofficial record the previous day but he could not improve on Curtiss's effort.

Moore-Brabazon's aeroplane, built not by the Wrights or Shorts, but by the Voisin Brothers.

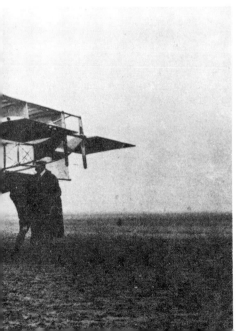

Disappointment followed disappointment for the Wrights for, on 24 August, when flying was again not possible until 5pm, Hubert Latham was succeeded on the course by Blériot who 'flew grandly' to establish a record of 46.18mph. Lefebvre could not match this, let alone exceed it, in an otherwise daring performance. A close challenge by Curtiss during the Gordon–Bennett Cup Race could not prevent Blériot from winning on 28 August with 47.83mph.

Earlier in 1909, in Britain, Alliott Verdon Roe had flown his Roe I triplane for all of 900 feet on 23 July. He followed this with a flight of half-a-mile on his Roe II triplane on 24 December. But it was still Cody who did most of Britain's flying, with a seven mile flight in his 'III' in August, and a forty-mile flight in September – the first flight of more than an hour in Britain.

When the *Daily Mail* offered a prize of £1000 for the first flight over a one-mile circuit by a Briton flying a British-built machine, the prize almost inevitably fell to J.T.C. Moore-Brabazon on 30 October, flying a Short-built Wright biplane, fitted with ailerons. In late April and early May of that year, Moore-Brabazon had made a

A Green engine of 1911, but little different from those used on early Short Brothers aircraft.

Alliott Verdon Roe
initially concentrated
on triplanes, con-
verting his original
biplanes. This is his
first triplane designed
as such, which flew
for 900 feet on 23 July
1909.

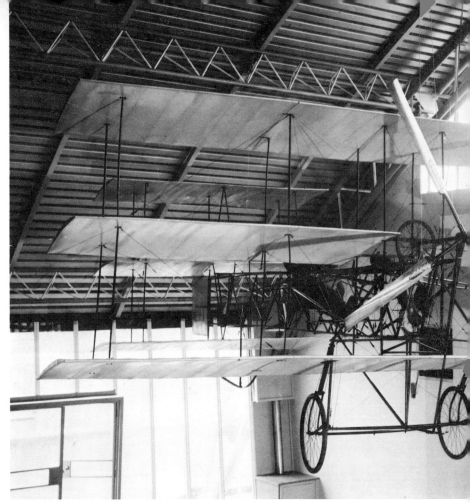

The first properly
qualified woman
pilot, Madame la
Baroness de la Roche,
sitting rather uneasily
in the pilot's seat of
her Voisin biplane.

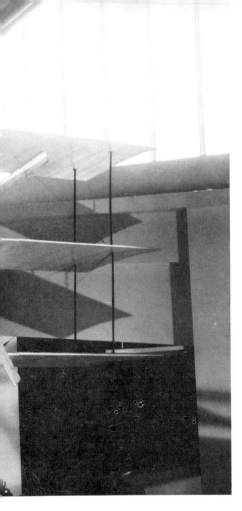

number of very short flights in Britain in a Voisin biplane, 'The Bird of Passage'. A number of firms were undertaking to build aircraft in Britain to the owner's design, and the Moore-Brabazon Short-Wright was the second such aircraft to be built, another going to the Hon. Charles Rolls of Rolls-Royce fame. However, the Committee on Imperial Defence ignored these developments and decided to stop building aircraft at Farnborough – which was costing just £2000 a year – in favour of spending £45,000 on airship development.

In France, Madame la Baronesse de la Roche, flying a Voisin biplane, became the first woman to qualify as a pilot.

From the time the Wrights arrived on the French scene to the time that the French surpassed their achievements at Reims was a mere twelve months – such was the rate of progress in aviation. The tables had been turned. The leading position held by the Wrights had been seized by those able to build upon their experience, while they themselves may have been blind to necessary improvements, for such is always the fate of the innovator. Yet in their turn the French, too, would be challenged by the, as then, backward British and Germans.

A close-up of Grade in his biplane.

4

THE MILITARY
TAKES AN INTEREST

**Accidents and doubts, the Wrights
win and lose, origins of naval
aviation, Fabre, Maurice Farman,
Rolls, De Havilland, Dunne,
Moisant, Chavez, Ely**

'Remember, one hour's flight is guaranteed with every "Cody Flyer" '
(*1910 advertisement for Cody Flying School*)

Madame Blériot's fears for her husband's safety had not been without substance. Flying at the end of 1909 in a high wind at Constantinople, ever anxious to please his public, Louis Blériot crashed into a row of houses, wrecking his aircraft. Fortunately, he only sustained minor injuries himself. He was in good company: on Christmas Eve, Alliott Verdon Roe damaged his second triplane in an accident.

Unhappily, these accidents at the end of 1909 proved to be ill-omens for the coming year. In 1910 no less than thirty pilots and two passengers were to lose their lives. This was to be the cost of flying's new popularity: during 1910 more than twenty aviation meetings were held in Europe, the most important at Nice and Milan, and three in the U.S.A.

Aeronautical progress continued to be steady, although a league table of Euro-

The British were not slow to have their own aeronautical exhibitions, even if it meant sharing space with motor boats!

pean Government air fleets at the onset of 1910 showed that a number of interesting comparisons could be made. Germany had no less than fourteen dirigibles and five aeroplanes. The French had only seven dirigibles but twenty-nine aeroplanes! Against this, the United Kingdom could boast just two of each. Even poor Tsarist Russia could muster three dirigibles and six aeroplanes. Italy and Austria were able to outdo the British effort.

On 4 January the first tragedy struck the world of aviation: the renowned French pioneer, Léon Delagrange was killed during a flight at Bordeaux, in front of a large crowd at the Croix d'Hins Aerodrome. According to *The Times* of London: 'He was making a turn against a wind which blew at the rate of 24 feet per second, when the left wing of his Blériot monoplane broke, and the other collapsed. M. Delagrange fell from a height of about 36 feet, fracturing his skull.' The paper felt moved to comment that this was 'the third fatal accident to a French aviator during the last four weeks'.

Doubts began to be expressed over the safety of aviation generally, and of monoplanes in particular. An accident to Alberto Santos-Dumont, although not fatal, had made some observers uneasy

Antoinette mono-
plane, 1910 vintage, at
a time of internal
strife in the concern,
during which both
Levavasseur and
Gastambide absented
themselves from the
firm.

A Blackburn mono-
plane on the Com-
pany's stand at the
Olympia Show.

about the monoplane. Hastily, the engineer who had assembled Delagrange's aircraft explained to the press that he was unable to account for the accident. The aircraft was the same as that used by Delagrange at Blackpool for a flight of nearly 55mph. Once the hysteria died down, the experts came up with a perfectly logical explanation – the Blériot XI's 18hp Anzani engine had been replaced by a power unit of no less than 40hp! It was hardly a good time for the Lebaudy Brothers to announce their intention to build aeroplanes.

However, progress was not hindered too seriously by popular doubts and fears. Dunne's latest aeroplane was on display at Eastchurch, powered by a 50–60hp Green engine and attracting much attention as 'the most remarkable and interesting machine yet constructed, for it is tailless and without an elevator, being designed to have natural stability'. Control was in fact effected by hinged flaps on the mainplanes.

By this time the wartime potential of the aeroplane was becoming apparent. On 14 January, in the United States, Glenn Curtiss took Lieutenant Paul Beck up to drop sandbags, representing bombs, on dummy targets from a height of 250 feet – missing each target by between 15 and 25 feet! Louis Paulhan flew in his Henri Farman to a height of 900 feet over Los Angeles, and speculated afterwards on the possibility of lifting a 375lb load of

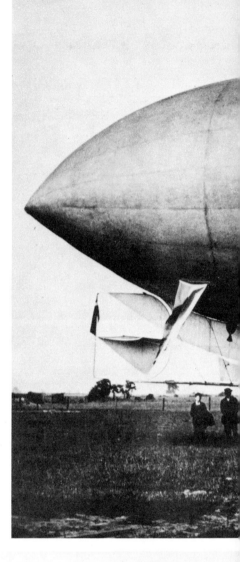

The English newspaper, the *Morning Post*, organised a public subscription to buy an airship for the British Army. A Lebaudy design, the so-called 'Morning Post' airship took to the air in September 1910.

dynamite to 10,000 feet if the aircraft were fitted with a more powerful motor. Of more immediate note, Paulhan, while still in Los Angeles, made one of the first flights with two passengers.

Dirigibles were receiving increasing attention at this time. The new British Army airship, Dirigible No. IIA, or 'Beta', made a flight on 12 February, under the control of Colonel Capper and Lieutenant Waterlow, manoeuvring over Laffan's Plain, which must go down in history as the British equivalent of Kitty Hawk. In June, again under Capper's direction, the Beta made a notable flight by British standards, leaving Aldershot at 11.39am on Friday, 3 June, flying to London and returning to Aldershot at 3.43pm.

At about the same time as the Beta was making her early voyages, a private enterprise rival built by E.T. Willows appeared at Cardiff. This was the first all-British dirigible, the Willows airship. It used a 30hp eight-cylinder J.A.P. engine to drive two propellers. In July it flew from Cardiff to London, a journey some four times the length of the Beta's.

Adventure and ambition were the keynotes of this period of aeronautical history. There was adventure in one of the first dirigible night flights by the Spanish 'España'; ambition was shown in the raising of 312,000 francs (£12,600), by a fund started in France to buy a replacement for the ill-fated 'La République'. The idea of a fund for airship purchase was not entirely French, however, for the London newspaper, the *Morning Post*, had prompted such a fund. Indeed, the

A British design, this is the Willows airship, 'City of Cardiff'.

'*Morning Post* airship', a semi-rigid built by the Lebaudy brothers at La Villette to the design of their engineer, M. Juilliott, actually took to the air in September.

One of the most ambitious ventures in 1910 was the establishment of the world's first airship services in Germany. In spite of the cynical attitude of contemporary aeronautical journals, the German airships were to carry 35,000 passengers without serious mishap before the outbreak of World War I.

After Reims Week and the immense public interest aroused by the occasion, aeronautics could only become respectable and fashionable. On 15 February, the Aero Club of the United Kingdom received His Majesty's permission to become the 'Royal Aero Club'. The London Air Show, which opened at Olympia on 19 March, enjoyed the attendance of the Prince and Princess of Wales – driven to the show from Marlborough House by the Hon. Charles Rolls in one of his famous cars. Whether or not His Royal Highness thought of buying an aeroplane is not recorded, but certainly Rolls himself seems to have been unable to resist the temptation to buy yet another aeroplane – he already had Short Brothers' and French-built versions of the Wright A. This time he bought a Roger Sommer, generally thought to be the best aeroplane at the Show.

The variety of aircraft on show was considerable. Apart from the Roger Sommer already mentioned, there were genuine and replica Demoiselles, the new Handley-Page Monoplane and the latest Roe triplane, and a Star monoplane which possessed the unusual feature of a flexible trailing edge. There were also Humber, Howard Wright (one of the first British manufacturers and no relation to the Wright brothers), Lane, Spere-Stirling and Farman designs.

In spite of the overall mood of optimism in the aeronautical world, which was displayed in successful events like the London Show, there were signs that not everything was as it should be. The Antoinette concern, for example, was desperately trying to recover from an internal policy dispute, and Léon Levavasseur

Gliders were not completely neglected at this time; this is the Clarke biplane glider.

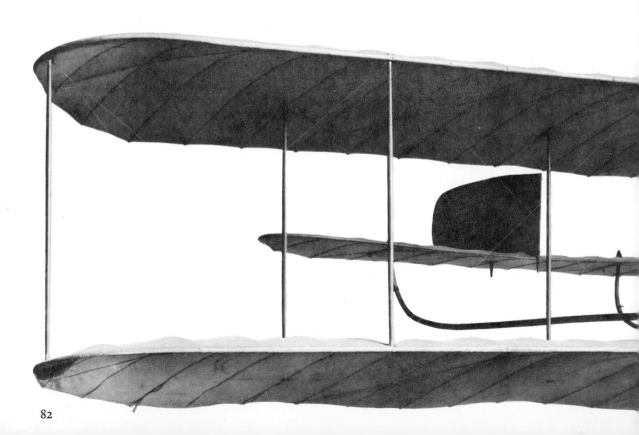

and Gastambide only returned to the Board in March after five months' absence.

A happier sign was the appearance of an all-British design by Captain Geoffrey de Havilland. The De Havilland No. 1 biplane was purchased by the British Government, together with the services of its designer. This connection was to last for several years, although the first aircraft was barely a success.

Then too, Orville Wright was 'practically unhurt' after his aircraft 'came down rapidly from 100 feet' during an exhibition flight at Montgomery, Alabama. This narrow escape could certainly be accounted good news. More sadly, the Wright brothers were now falling behind fast in the aeronautical race, although they did produce a series of racing biplanes with some success before the year ended. These were the Wright 'Model R' and

The famous illusionist, Houdini, seated in the cockpit of his Voisin biplane during 1910, the year he learnt to fly and started to fulfil a number of dates for exhibition flights, although he did not attempt aerobatics.

Houdini in his Voisin, probably after take-off.

the smaller 'Baby Wright' and 'Baby Grand', and marked the first use by the Wrights of the wheeled undercarriage and the dropping of the forward elevator. At the same time, a wheeled successor to the 'A', the 'B' had also appeared, although the U.S. Army's first 'B' had been delivered with skids in late 1909.

Faced with the start of a downturn in their ability to be in the forefront of aeronautical development, no doubt the Wrights were relieved at the outcome of the court cases over their patents in the U.S. These actions had involved the Wrights' alleging infringement of their patents by Glenn Curtiss and Louis Paulhan. Judge Hazel stated plainly enough in his summing up that, 'upon this contention it is sufficient to say that the affidavits for the complainants so clearly define the principle of invention of the flying machine in question that I am reasonably satisfied.' So the Curtiss and Paulhan cases were settled for the time being – although appeals would involve Curtiss in extensive alteration of the Langley 'Aerodrome A', so that a flight could be made in 1914 with this aircraft in a final attempt to disprove the Wrights' case. Paulhan received some consolation for his defeat when he won

Houdini in flight.

Major Baden-Powell, brother of the founder of the Boy Scout movement, experimented with gliders before building this small powered glider the Midge.

The Honourable Charles Rolls, founder with Henry Royce of the famous motor manufacturer, and a pioneer aviator. Rolls made the first return flight across the English Channel in 1910, but within a month was killed in a flying accident at Bournemouth.

the £10,000 *Daily Mail* prize for a London-to-Manchester flight. He beat the Englishman Claude Grahame-White into second place, although both men used Henri Farman biplanes.

The British were now well aware of the possibilities of the aeroplane. Captain Scott, visiting Bristol on 21 April, shortly before setting off for his ill-fated Antarctic expedition, was offered the use of an aeroplane. He graciously declined, however, saying that 'the possibilities were most interesting'. If Scott had known that a Frenchman, Henri Fabre, had flown a frail, but nevertheless the first, floatplane at Marseilles on 28 March, he might have thought the possibilities to be more interesting still. However, his expedition was to experience much trouble with their motor-sledges, preferring dog-sledges, and it is hardly likely that the early internal combustion engine would have done better in an aeroplane in the rigours of the Antarctic climate.

The famous illusionist, Houdini, started to fly in the spring of 1910, in a Voisin biplane. There was no element of illusion in Roger Sommer's feat of taking up no less than three passengers on one of his own aircraft for a flight of five miles over

the French village of Remilly.

Night flying obviously had to be established before the full practical potential of the aeroplane could be realised. The hazards were daunting, especially the loss of horizon, so important to the pilot. Grahame-White is supposed to have made a take-off before dawn during the London-to-Manchester race, but the first real attempt at night flight was made by a Frenchman, Aubrun, flying a Blériot XI in Argentina on 10 March. Grahame-White made the first night flight in Europe on 28 April. Some considerable thought had to be given to the problems of navigation at night. By the end of the year the French were experimenting with large illuminated figures, 1.75 metres high, and assessing their value from the top of the Eiffel Tower.

Another problem which began to receive more attention at this time was that of training. Maurice Farman had still to build his famous Longhorn. This was a biplane, so called because of the extravagant sweep forward and upward of the landing skids, which afforded some protection to the aircraft in the event of a messy landing. Henri Farman visited his brother's works and was given a flight in a predecessor of the Longhorn. Of the two

The British Army's 'Baby' airship, built by the simple expedient of fitting an aeroplane-type fuselage to an airship.

The star of the Antoinette stable at Nice was, as usual, the Englishman, Hubert Latham, who was forced, not for the first time, to ditch his aircraft.

Opposite:
The first big aviation meeting of 1910 was held at Nice, in the spring. This is a much exaggerated artistic impression!

brothers, Maurice was the more practical if less exciting. During the summer, the Cody and Grahame-White flying schools were set up, extending the opportunities for would-be aviators to acquire flying skills.

At the beginning of June, the Hon.

Charles Rolls flew one of his Wright A biplanes on a return trip across the English Channel, giving his country this one first at least. The event was seized upon by an enthusiastic press, which quickly made the point that a Frenchman might have flown the Channel, but that

MILANO
CIRCUITO AEREO
INTERNAZIONALE
24 SETT^{bre}–3 OTT^{bre} 1910
PREMI L.300000

Another major event of 1910 was the Milan meeting, and it was while flying over the Alps to this event that Chavez crashed, and was fatally injured.

Less illustrious than the Nice or Milan meetings was one of the first major British aeronautical meetings, held at Doncaster, which produced little worthwhile flying.

an Englishman had flown across and back again. It was an opportune moment for the people of Cambrai, Louis Blériot's birthplace, to unveil in his presence a monument commemorating his achievement.

Poor Rolls did not have long in which to savour his successes. On 12 July, he took part in a flying display at Bournemouth. Flying at just 50 feet into the wind, but diving slightly to maintain speed, he tried to pull his aircraft's nose up. The crowd heard the sound of splitting wood as part of the tailplane and rudder broke away, before the aircraft rolled over and plunged a final 30 feet upside down to the ground. Witnesses described the sound of the crash as appalling, and it was followed by an explosion from the motor. At the inquest, the jury returned the verdict that: 'Mr Rolls lost his life by concussion and laceration to the brain owing to a fall from a biplane.'

It remained for an attempt to be made

on a Paris-to-London flight, and this was tried by a Frenchman, Moisant. He took off in his Blériot monoplane at 5pm on Tuesday, 17 August, accompanied by his mechanic, Fileux. The journey was completed in stages. Moisant landed at Amiens at 7.30 on the first night, and took off at 10.45am the next morning for the actual Channel crossing, flying through a stiff breeze to land at Tilmanstone, near Walmer in Kent, at 11.25am. Further flying was left to the next day. The aircraft set off at 5am for a 65-minute flight over Canterbury to Sittingbourne. From here the second stage of the day started at 9.30am and ended in a crash landing on an allotment near Rainham in which the propeller was damaged. Even with help from Short Brothers, it was Saturday before a new propeller from France arrived and could be fitted. Hardly impatient, Moisant then flew to Gillingham, where high winds detained him until Monday, 23 August, when he took off to fly to Wrotham, where he was to refuel. But he failed to clear the Otford Hills and finally crash-landed at Kemsing, near Sevenoaks. This was not the only epic flight to end in disappointment, and the one which followed had a more tragic outcome.

The Milan Aviation Meeting in September was seized upon by a Peruvian, Chavez, as an opportunity to win the £4000 prize offered for the first trans-Alpine flight. He waited seven days for favourable conditions, before taking off from Brigue in his Blériot monoplane at 13.30 hours on Friday, 23 September. Flying up the Simplon Pass, he enjoyed a fairly smooth flight until he reached the Gorge of Gondo, where his aircraft was buffeted so fiercely that his watch was torn from his wrist. The American pioneer, Charles Weyman, who was following him, gave up as his aircraft could not make altitude. Barometer trouble had forced Chavez to abandon an attempt to cross the Alps by the Mouncern Pass.

However, all went well until he came in to land on the Italian side of the Alps at Domodossola, where either he miscalculated or his aircraft failed him, and he crashed. Poor Chavez was removed from the wreckage, half conscious, murmuring, 'C'est terrible!' and 'Oh! Mes

FIRST AVIATION
MEETING IN ENGLAND.

CODY
DELAGRANGE
FARMAN
SOMMER
LEBLON
MOLON
PREVOT
DE LA VAUX
& OTHER
AVIATORS ENGAGED.

DONCASTER
15TH TO 23RD OCTOBER
1909.

Go by train! Even Doncaster was value for day trippers.

amis!' He was rushed to hospital, and at first seemed to be recovering from his injuries, which included fractures to both legs, but the shock proved to be too great, and he died suddenly on the Tuesday.

The Milan meeting, although less of an event than Reims, was a success, in spite of these problems. Even Reims in 1910 attracted less attention than it had done in 1909 – possibly because the politicians and others who had done so much to contribute to the success of the 1909 meeting were by this time wrestling with more practical problems.

In addition to their small army air arms, both Britain and France had formed naval aeronautical detachments. Like the British Army's 'Nulli Secundus', the first naval airship, named appropriately enough 'Navy Airship No. 1' or 'Mayfly', was doomed to failure. In fact it collapsed after completion at Barrow-in-Furness because the structure had been dangerously weakened by attempts to lighten it. The French, who started the Service Aéronautique with a Henri Farman and a Voisin, and supplemented these with Blériot and Nieuport types, fared better.

Nevertheless, the Royal Navy had in some ways a more enlightened approach to heavier-than-air flight than its land-orientated counterpart, which had been happy to fall in line with official directives to favour aerostation rather than aviation. The Royal Aero Club put two Short biplanes, based at Eastchurch, at the disposal of officers of the Royal Navy who wished to learn to fly. Admiral Sir C.C. Drury, Commander-in-Chief at the Nore, drew the attention of his officers to the availability of these aircraft: 'biplanes of the most modern type, fitted with Gnome motors, and placed at the disposal of naval officers at all times and without charge.' Indeed, the only two conditions attached to use of these aircraft were that any damage should be made good, and that the officers using them should become Royal Aero Club members. King George V even approved an Order in Council giving a daily allowance to naval airmen of six shillings for officers, half-a-crown for N.C.O.s, and two shillings for able seamen.

In marked contrast to all this official encouragement was an article in the

Lieutenant Eugene Ely, U.S.N., in the pilot's seat of his Curtiss biplane before making his historic flight from the cruiser, U.S.S. *Birmingham*, in November 1910.

The first Royal Navy airship, the Mayfly, appeared in 1910, and is seen here after completion.

Lancet advising aviators to keep to a low and steady altitude, for fear of upsetting their blood pressure. A writer to *Flight* warned that, in a future war, the crew of an enemy aircraft might feel inclined to drop bombs on a town or village from which they were shot at!

The real action was taking place in the United States at this time. While McCurdy, a Canadian colleague of Curtiss, was waiting to fly his Curtiss biplane from a platform built over the bows of the Hamburg–America liner *Pennsylvania*, a young U.S. Navy officer,

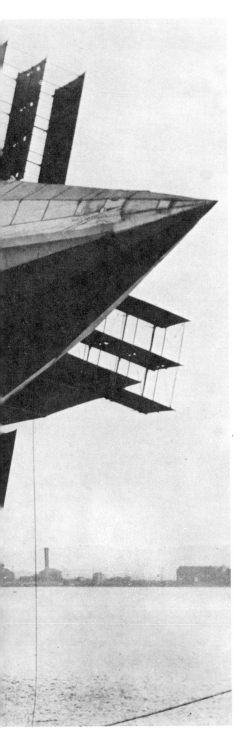

20 knots into the wind. Impatient, Ely had other ideas, as soon as the anchor was raised at 15.16 hours, and during the short pause while the *Birmingham* got underway, he started the engine of his frail craft and gave the word for its release. He could not gather sufficient speed as he trundled forward along the 80-foot launching platform. The aircraft rolled off the end of the platform and made a powered glide for the sea, damaging the propeller, before Ely could gain both control and speed. In spite of this, Ely succeeded in flying to Willoughby Spit, just $2\frac{1}{2}$ miles away, where he landed safely. The crew of the *Birmingham* were enthusiastic spectators of this first flight from a ship – although the signal to the shore was short and matter-of-fact: 'Ely's just gone.'

Ely's successful flight, although he flew a rather shorter distance than he had intended, inspired the French. They began to consider plans for converting their cruiser *La Foudre* to handle aircraft, with a 125-foot-long launching platform. Indeed, the end of the year saw increasing military involvement in aviation development. The first Etrich Taubes were completed for the German Military Air Service; the Spanish were making preparations to build an air arm; and the Imperial Russian Flying Corps founded an Army flying school at Gatchiva and a Navy school at Sevastopol. The German dirigible services were obviously successful but the aeroplane, too, was beginning to play an important role in military thinking.

Unfortunately, the original specification of the Mayfly was altered to lighten the craft, which collapsed shortly afterwards as a result!

Lieutenant Eugene B. Ely, was waiting to fly his Curtiss biplane from the light cruiser, U.S.S. *Birmingham*. Ely actually had the support of Curtiss.

It was eventually decided that Ely's attempt should be made after lunch on 14 November, while his ship steamed at

5
SEAWARD

Ship take-offs and landings, seaplanes and amphibians, long distance flights, airmail, new techniques, Fokker, Wrights, De Havilland, Roe, Ely, Grahame-White

'When my brother and I built and flew the first man-carrying flying machine, we thought that we were introducing into the world an invention which would make further wars practically impossible.'
Orville Wright

The year 1910 had seen so many disasters in the world of aeronautics that 1911 could not but see an improvement in the situation. It was a year of continued development, with the appearance of a number of innovations as the early aviators struggled to make their still temperamental steeds into truly practical and reliable flying machines. Some of the achievements of the previous year provided a basis for development: these included night flying trials and McCurdy's experiments with sending and receiving radio messages while flying at Sheepshead Bay, New York. The new year was to see more night flying and more radio experiments, notably at Brooklands in England.

Naturally, many developments were not perfected in any one year. One obvious example of this was the first practical airspeed indicator, which was completed by the Frenchman, Captain A. Etévé, in late 1910, and underwent successful trials in January 1911. Perhaps one of the most important achievements to span the years 1910 and 1911 was the work of the young U.S. Navy officer, Lieutenant Eugene Ely, in shipboard aircraft operation. On 18 January 1910, Ely made the first landing by an aircraft onto a ship – the cruiser U.S.S. *Pennsylvania* lying at anchor in San Francisco Bay. This time, the decision to make the attempt while the ship was not underway was her commander's, Captain Pond, who felt that there was insufficient room to manoeuvre the *Pennsylvania* in the anchorage.

Ely's epic flight started at 10.45am from Selfridge Field, an Army Camp some 12 miles to the south of San Francisco. The *Pennsylvania* lay at anchor some 12 miles out in the Bay. Flying low over the city and out over the Bay, Ely could judge the ship's position by the sounding of her siren. He flew slowly past the cruiser and on for 'some hundreds of yards' before turning back. Taking his plane slowly upwards towards the stern of the vessel, Ely finally settled down on a platform built over the stern at 11.01am. His landing was arrested by the first primitive arrester wire system: wires were strung across the 50-foot-wide platform and kept in place by a 100lb sandbag at each end. The system worked well, and Ely needed only 60 feet

of the 130-foot-long platform to stop from a speed of about 40mph. According to one eyewitness account: 'The aeroplane, which was a Curtiss biplane, was hardly shaken by contact with the deck of the cruiser.'

The landing was announced by a triumphant blast on the *Pennsylvania's* siren, echoed by those of the other ships in the Bay and boosted by the enthusiastic cheers of their crews. Captain Pond entertained Ely to an early luncheon in his honour. Only an hour after landing he was again ready for take-off. The cruiser was still at anchor as Ely departed 'at high speed', this time making only a slight dip towards the water before climbing steadily and circling the ships in the Bay. He returned to Selfridge Field, flying over San Francisco at the then remarkable height of 2000 feet. On landing he was cheered by the officers of the 13th U.S. Infantry Regiment, in

The designer of the aircraft used by Ely, and the main force behind the not unrelated development of the hydro-aeroplane was, of course, none other than Glenn Curtiss.

training at the Field.

While the U.S. Navy was conducting these far-sighted experiments, Curtiss himself was directing his energies elsewhere. On 26 January 1911, he successfully tested the first practical float-plane at San Diego, California. This feat led a contemporary to declare that 'he had made the first significant advance in aviation since the Wright Brothers'. This must have been balm to his soul after the court decisions of the previous year. Curtiss followed this success in February by making the first flight from land to water. He landed his aircraft on the water before taking off again and returning to his starting point. In spite of this, the machine could not really be considered

as the first practical amphibian. Nevertheless, this new type of aeroplane was sufficiently developed by August for Hugh Robinson to be able to fly a Curtiss machine onto the surface of Lake Michigan, where he picked up the pilot of another aircraft which had ditched in the water.

Curtiss was not the only one interested in water landings. In France, on 3 August, according to a report in *The Times* of London the following morning: 'The airman Colliex flew from Issy-les-Moulineaux this morning on a biplane fitted with floats and descended on the Seine, where he stayed on the water and floated. After another flight from the land and descent on the water, the aero-

plane was taken in tow and brought to Issy.' His aircraft was a standard Voisin machine which had been modified by Fabre.

A Royal Navy officer, Lieutenant Oliver Schwann, bought an aeroplane at his own expense and fitted it with floats and gas bags. He was able to make a water take-off with this machine in November 1911, while a fellow officer, Lieutenant Arthur M. Longmore, R.N., flew a Short S.27 biplane, fitted with airbags for the purpose, onto the River Medway on 1 December, and shortly afterwards succeeded in taking off again.

Longmore was one of the Royal Navy's first four pilots under the Royal Aero Club's scheme. The others were Lieu-

One of the first epic long-distance flights was that of the American, Calbraith Rodgers, in a Wright EX biplane from Long Island to Long Beach – right across the United States – in September to November, 1911. He took 82 flying hours and 49 days, with 19 crashes so that little of the original aircraft remained on reaching his destination.

Calbraith Rodgers.

tenant Charles Rumney Samson, R.N., Lieutenant R. Gregory, R.N., and Lieutenant E.L. Gerrard, R.M.L.I. Others followed. One of them, who became a pilot in 1911, Sub-Lieutenant F.E.T. Hewlett, R.N., had the distinction of being the first man to be taught to fly by his mother – a woman of determined character who flew in wet weather wearing sabots, a type of wooden clog.

The Canadian, McCurdy, joined the other marine aviators and flew from Key West, off the Florida Coast, to Havana in Cuba, a distance over water of some 90 miles. At the time this was a record for flight over water, when most such flights were still cross-Channel!

While the United States Navy had been pre-occupied with its experiments at San Francisco, the United States Army

was conducting the first live bombing tests from a Wright biplane in the same location. Lieutenant Riley Scott of the U.S. Army produced the first bomb sight at this time.

There was progress elsewhere, too. A new air speed record of 69.48mph was made by the Frenchman, Alfred Leblanc, flying a Blériot monoplane on 12 April. But this was also to be the year of the long-distance aviator. The first non-stop London to Paris flight was made in a Blériot by an aviator named Prier, chief instructor at the Blériot Flying School at Hendon. In Prier's own words: 'I left Hendon at 1.37pm, and, passing Boulogne at 3.13pm, I arrived at Issy-les-Moulineaux at 5.33pm, so that I was exactly 3 hours and 56 minutes in the air.'

This was a modest account of the trip.

Much of the flight had been conducted in thick mist, and after Prier had flown over Chatham and Canterbury, past Dover to Calais, and then followed the railway line to Boulogne, Abbéville and Beauvais, the fog became so bad that he failed to see the Eiffel Tower as he passed it. The distance of 226 miles was covered at an average speed of 62mph. Blériot attributed Prier's success to his habit of flying high to avoid wind eddies near to the ground.

Many other long-distance flights were connected with air races, such as the one between Paris and Madrid, which was won by Védrines flying a new Morane monoplane. Blériot aircraft flown by Conneau (alias André Beaumont) won the Paris-to-Rome and the Paris–Brussels–London–Amiens–Paris races. McCurdy

won the Hamilton-to-Toronto race in his native Canada using an American Curtiss biplane.

Possibly the most interesting feature of these long-distance flights was the re-emergence of the Wright aircraft. In August, Atwood flew a Wright biplane from St Louis to New York via Chicago, covering no less than 1260 miles in a total flying time of just 28 hours 53 minutes. In September–November, Calbraith Rodgers flew in a special Wright EX biplane across the United States from Long Island to Long Beach, via Chicago and San Antonio. Although Rodgers covered the incredible distance of 4000 miles in just 82 flying hours, the flight required 82 stages and took all of 49 days. Rodgers crashed no less than 19 times! He was followed by a trainload of spares and it

The culmination of the work carried out by José Weiss in England, this dated flapping-wing glider probably had some influence on the design of the Handley Page 'Yellow Peril' monoplane of 1911.

Although many of the early aeroplanes had twin propellers, the first multi-engined aeroplane to fly was the Short 'Triple-Twin' of 1911, with three propellers, later reduced to two and the name changed to 'Tandem-Twin', as seen here.

is unlikely that there was much of the original structure remaining by the time he arrived in California.

From today's standpoint, these flights may give the impression of a fairly lighthearted approach to what was essentially a serious business. Events like Latham's crossing of the Golden Gate at San Francisco on 7 January in an Antoinette, and Lincoln Beachey's flight over Niagara Falls and under the nearby suspension bridge in a Curtiss biplane on 28 June, contribute to this impression. But official aeronautical circles took these occurrences seriously. In March there was dispute, mainly between the Aéro Club de France and the Royal Aero Club, over the award to the Count de Lesseps of the $10,000 prize for the first flight round the Statue of Liberty. The R.A.C. protested against the decision, but the Fédération Aéronautique Internationale

had already disqualified the Englishman, Claud Grahame-White, and the Frenchman, Moisant, the former for fouling Pylon No. 5 during his attempt.

Airship development was not particularly significant at this time, although national fleets of these monsters were expanding. Passengers continued to be carried steadily and peacefully across Germany, at heights and speeds which made the most of the landscapes, and townscapes, over which they passed.

It was, however, a time of revived interest in the glider – largely through the activities of none other than the Wright brothers! The renewed glider experiments attracted widespread attention because the Wrights were known to have developed an automatic stabiliser: a 'balancing device which, it is believed, will be serviceable against strong winds. Details are being withheld until it is successfully tested.' This was in October at the Wright brothers' old testing ground in the Kill Devil Hills. Orville Wright was reported as saying: 'Before we leave here we hope to demonstrate that the glider can be held in a fixed position in the air for five minutes or more.'

The new Wright glider differed greatly from its predecessors in certain fundamental points. It not only had a rear rudder, but a rear-mounted elevator as well, with a 10lb sandbag placed eight feet in front on a pole. And it worked! On 26 October *The Times* of London reported:

Mr. Orville Wright rode his glider for 9¾ minutes in the teeth of a 50 mile wind at Kill Devil Hill yesterday.

The glider is equipped with a rear rudder 24 square feet in area and ailerons. A 10 lb. sandbag was suspended at the end of a rod extending 8 feet in front of the seat. The glider started from the summit of a sand dune and, mounting successive gusts of wind like a ship over the waves, reached a height of 150 feet. Whenever the wind began to drive backward, Mr. Wright would make a dip, raising himself again by tilting the poles. For several minutes the glider was stabilising, while the wind blew through the canvas. A bird which was unable to

One of the Cody machines in the air over Laffan's Plain at Farnborough, probably in 1910 or 1911.

make headway against the gale perched exhausted upon one of the wires, and the airman reached out and caught it. The glider descended in a long and graceful curve.

Glider pioneers had been active throughout the early years of powered flight. In England, José Weiss, and in the United States, Professor John J. Montgomery, had persisted with glider design. Montgomery had started work as early as 1883, and had been absorbed in the possibilities for ornithoptering flight. In addition he had produced a number of fixed wing designs. He died late in 1911, while testing one of his own aircraft.

Weiss was attracted by the bird-form wing and by the outdated concept of inherent stability. He in fact inspired Handley-Page's early monoplane designs – the earliest of which, the 'Yellow Peril', first flew in 1911.

Another seeker after inherent stability at this time was the Dutchman, Anthony Fokker who, at the age of eighteen, built his first powered aircraft. This flew even though it lacked any means of control in roll, making up for this deficiency by acute dihedral.

It was in 1911 that structural techniques started to change. There was a movement away from the wood, canvas and wire of the early years; although this

process was not to gain real momentum until after World War I had ended. A year before the appearance of the famous Monocoque Deperdussin, but in the same year that the Swiss inventor, Ruchonnet, invented the concept, Léon Levavasseur embodied a rudimentary cantilever wing in his Monobloc Antoinette. The aircraft was far from successful, fitted with either a 50hp or a 100hp engine. Neither engine succeeded in lifting the machine off the ground for more than a few yards because the design remained heavy and underpowered. The

retractable undercarriage. Unfortunately this could do little to improve what was otherwise a mediocre aircraft. Short Brothers built the first twin-engined aircraft actually to fly, known as the Triple-Twin. It had an engine at each end of the fuselage nacelle, one driving two propellers and the other a single propeller. It was later modified as the Tandem-Twin with each engine driving a single airscrew.

The standard World War I fighter and reconnaissance aircraft was beginning to take shape in A.V. Roe's 1912 biplane. This was the predecessor of the Avro 504 biplane, and the B.E.1, built at Farnborough by F.M. Green and Captain Geoffrey de Havilland. These were biplanes with single tractor propellers and the now traditional tailplane configuration. It was at this time too that the Army Balloon Factory at Farnborough adopted the more appropriate title of the Army Aircraft Factory.

It was another Farnborough product, the S.E.1. biplane, which killed the Assistant Superintendent of the Factory, Lieutenant T. Ridge, in an early instance of a spin. Although it was to be a while before this type of accident became known and could be mastered, a little later that same year, another Englishman, Frederick Raynham, managed to recover from a spin accidentally after his Avro biplane had stalled while climbing through heavy fog.

New manufacturers mushroomed. Apart from the early Deperdussin factory, others interested in building monoplanes at this time included the Albatros, Bristol, Breguet, Hanriot and Morane factories, and Vickers, hitherto a shipbuilder and airship manufacturer.

Practical development continued side by side with displays of aeronautical exhibitionism. A good example of the latter was the mania for getting as many passengers as possible into the air in one aeroplane. This was more of a 'student in telephone box' stunt than a practical step forward. A special Blériot took off with ten passengers and, on another occasion, a Breguet struggled into the skies with eleven passengers. Eventually a special Roger Sommer managed to carry thirteen passengers. The passengers literally had to hang on, and in order to boost

Monobloc Antoinette in fact showed many of the symptoms of having been designed in haste.

Other developments emerged at this time as well. The first oleo-sprung undercarriage appeared, and the German Wiencziers monoplane had a very basic

One of the most significant aircraft in aeronautical history, the B.E.1 biplane built at Farnborough in 1911 by F.M. Green and Geoffrey de Havilland. This machine, with a Roe biplane of the following year, pointed the way for the World War I scout aircraft and the biplane revival.

The Avro (Alliott Verdon Roe) biplane of 1911 marked Roe's return to the biplane design, and was an interim step for a more successful aircraft on which the Avro name was to be firmly established.

the numbers these attempts usually included a few children. There was no practical significance either in the first air cargo flight, which was something of a publicity stunt for the British General Electric Company. A Valkyrie monoplane carried a consignment of lightbulbs from Shoreham to nearby Hove in Sussex, England, on 4 July 1911.

This was the year of the first airmail flights, if one discounts the balloon mail at the Siege of Paris in 1870. As a part of the celebrations connected with the Coronation of King George V, the pilots of the Blériot and Grahame-White flying schools at Hendon initiated a regular airmail service from Hendon to Windsor, a distance of eleven miles. This lasted from 9 September until 26 September. In the United States, on 23 September, Earl L.

Ovington carried a quantity of mail in his Blériot monoplane from Garden City to Mineola, a distance of only six miles.

But official distrust of the aeroplane was still such that flying was banned over London and Windsor at the time of King George V's Coronation. Some of this distrust seems to have been directed at the aviators themselves. General Rocques, head of the French Military Aviation Department, decided that the qualifying requirements for a pilot's certificate awarded by the Aéro Club de France were not strict enough. By this time the Aéro Club de France had issued 354 certificates, compared with the Royal Aero Club's 55. He stipulated that officers wishing to serve as aviators would be required to make a flight of at least 100 kilometres across country; of more than

two hours duration; a flight of at least 300 metres altitude (about 1000 feet); and one of at least ten metres per second. This set of stipulations does not seem to have deterred would-be pilots for, on 24 October, it was announced that, 'Seven pilots of the French Army executed simultaneous and successful flights this morning on Blériot aeroplanes from the aerodrome at Etampes to the camp at Satany. The flights were undertaken as part of their examination for the technical certificate. They intend to fly back to Etampes this evening.'

Military interest in aviation continued to be keen. The year had seen a 'Concours Militaire' at the Reims Aviation Meeting, and a number of experiments in fitting a machine gun to aircraft. The 23 October saw the first military operational use of heavier-than-air, powered flight: Lieutenant Piazzi of the Italian Army flew a reconnaissance mission in a Nieuport monoplane against the Turkish Army. He found the Turks at an oasis some 12 miles from Tripoli, over which he flew at low height to the excitement of the inhabitants. Italy and Turkey, needless to say, were at war. The Turks in their turn were quick to order German and French aircraft and to recruit foreign pilots, thus gaining for Turkey the distinction of having the longest history of military aviation of any Middle Eastern power.

The young Anthony Fokker, at only 18, designed and built this monoplane, lacking any means of control in roll, but using excessive dihedral to maintain stability.

6
FORGING AHEAD

Catapults, automatic pilots, amphibians, flying-boats, trainers, the airship threat, build-up of air power, biplane progress, Maurice Farman, Curtiss, Schneider, Védrines, Samson, Wilbur Wright

'I am bound to confess that my imagination supplied me at every moment with the most realistic anticipations of a crash . . . we descended in due course with perfect safety. I have no compunction in relating the apprehensions which surrounded my first taste of the glorious sensations of flying. I am sure that when the secrets of all hearts are revealed, they will be found to have been shared by a good many others. I continued to fly on every possible occasion when my other duties permitted.'

Sir Winston Churchill
(writing of his first flight, 1912)

The most significant characteristic of aviation in 1912 was the amount of official interest now taken in the aeroplane. The 'Concours Militaire' at Reims in October 1911; the flights by Ely and other pioneers of naval and military aviation; the trials with bombs and machine guns; all had helped to expand the scope of military and naval aviation. From this point there was no turning back; the aeroplane had been conscripted as an instrument of war.

Once again the first honours of the year went to a naval aviator – but this time he was British. A Royal Navy pilot, Lieutenant Charles Rumney Samson, was preparing to make the first aeroplane flight from a British warship, the battleship, H.M.S. *Africa*. It was to be the first of several successes in 1912 by naval aeroplanes and hydro-aeroplanes.

The 10 January dawned grey and misty at the Royal Aero Club's airfield at Eastchurch, on the Isle of Sheppey, and flying was impossible until late in the morning. At noon, Lieutenant Samson climbed into the same Short S. 27 biplane which had served Longmore so well in the preceding December. He took off for the short flight to Cockleshell Hard. As soon as he landed there a well-rehearsed plan got underway. The aircraft was manhandled into a lighter and then towed by a pinnace out to H.M.S. *Africa*.

A second battleship, H.M.S. *Hibernia*, was converted to launch aircraft during the 1912 Annual Review of the Fleet, and from this ship Lieutenant Charles Rumney Samson made the first take-off from a vessel underway.

The battleship's derrick lifted the frail machine onto the launching platform constructed over the forecastle.

It had never been intended that the *Africa* should be underway at the time of the take-off attempt. Instead, at 14.20, while the ship lay at anchor in Sheerness Harbour, the aircraft's 50hp Gnome rotary engine was started. After a short run forward, the S.27 climbed steadily, flying over the destroyer, H.M.S. *Cherwell* and back again over H.M.S. *Africa* to the cheers of the ship's company. It then flew along the Medway to West Minster and arrived back over Eastchurch at an altitude of 800 feet.

Samson's aircraft was fitted with airbags in case an emergency landing on the river was necessary – a safety feature which reputedly 'heartened' his admiral.

Some accounts, including certain official publications, credit Samson with a shipboard take-off in the previous December, but there appears to be no evidence to support this and other official accounts regard the well-documented and reported flight of 10 January as his first attempt. Samson had, however, attempted a water take-off on 28 November but crashed on landing.

The trend away from the monoplane to the biplane was growing rapidly. Avro produced the first cabin aircraft, a biplane, later in the year, but in the meantime also produced an improved biplane with ailerons, paving the way for the highly successful 504 biplane trainer. The Army Aircraft Factory – which changed its name yet again in April to the Royal Aircraft Factory – produced an improved version of its B.E.1 tractor biplane, the B.E.2. It followed this with the B.S.1, a

Naval aviators were again to the fore in 1912 when, on 10 January, Lieutenant Charles Rumney Samson flew this Short S.27 biplane from the battleship H.M.S. *Africa*, anchored off Sheerness.

Shorts soon graduated to building the more fashionable tractor biplane. No doubt development was encouraged by the enthusiastic support of the First Lord of the Admiralty, Winston Churchill. The aircraft shown, an S.41, first appeared in 1912, and it is seen here with Samson acting as pilot for Churchill.

The glider pioneers of this period failed to advance their art significantly, and were easily eclipsed by the more exciting powered machines. An unusual glider was this biplane flown by the Englishman, Richards, at Kirby Lonsdale in November 1912.

100hp Gnome-powered biplane designed by Geoffrey de Havilland, which paved the way for the first true scout and fighter aircraft in World War I. Aircraft such as the B.S.1 – a trendsetter with a maximum speed of 92mph, combined with robust construction, good streamlining and excellent manoeuvrability – did much to emphasise the superiority of the biplane over the monoplane.

One of the problems of the monoplane was still the need for a fairly large wing area, which gave rise to structural problems not encountered in the more compact biplane. Indeed the drag of the forest of bracing wires needed for the monoplane's wings at the time more than outweighed the drag inherent in a good biplane design.

Yet, in spite of the steps forward in biplane development, the next real technical innovation came with a monoplane – the so-called Monocoque Deperdussin. The monocoque form of construction was the invention of Ruchonnet, a Swiss living in France. It differed from what might be described as the traditional form of aircraft construction in that the skin or shell of the fuselage bore the load, rather than a canvas-covered wood or steel framework. The Monocoque Deperdussin aeroplane was designed by Armand Deperdussin's chief designer, Bechereau. It had a wooden fuselage, of modern appearance, and its 140hp Gnome rotary engine was partially enclosed. By comparison, even the Blériots and

After working in secret at Blair Atholl, in Scotland, J. W. Dunne took this aircraft to Eastchurch. It can be fairly described as the first working tail-less aircraft.

Avro can have had little idea of the success which awaited the 504 design – indeed, it may have been considered a failure in some ways since it was originally intended to be a scout, but proved too slow, and so became one of the first true training-aircraft.

Further development of the basic B.E.1 soon led to the B.E.2, marking a further step towards the scout aircraft of World War I.

Even more significant than the B.E.2, and from the same stable, the Royal Aircraft Factory, as the Army Aircraft Factory was now called, was the B.S.1 biplane, powered by a 100hp Gnome rotary engine and designed by Geoffrey de Havilland. This is the first B.S.1 being prepared for a flight from Farnborough.

Antoinettes seemed dated.

The Monocoque Deperdussin reigned supreme as the world air-speed record-holder for the remainder of the period up to the outbreak of World War I – and, in fact, through the war as well since the official speed record was suspended for the duration of hostilities. The first of the Deperdussin's records was established at Pau, in the South of France on 13 January 1912, when Jules Védrines flew the aircraft to a then-record speed of more than 90mph. Other records followed; the aircraft was taken past the 100mph mark by Védrines on 22 February, and it won the Gordon–Bennett Cup Race at Chicago on 9 September with a record for the year of 108mph.

It was at a dinner held after the 1912 Gordon–Bennett Cup Race that a wealthy, young Frenchman presented a prize to be competed for annually by hydro-aeroplanes – which he considered to have been neglected and which he believed would be able to achieve the highest speeds. His name, of course, was Jacques Schneider.

Another monoplane doing well at this time was the small Morane–Saulnier, which had a Gnome engine of just 50hp. This aircraft established a two hour distance record of 147 miles on 1 March. The pilot was Tabuteau. Later in the year, an altitude record of 18,405 feet was set by a Morane–Saulnier. A biplane scored a success when a Maurice Farman set the 1912 endurance record of 628 miles.

Other designers tried to emulate the Monocoque Deperdussin's success, and even to improve upon it. Reissner's corrugated aluminium wings for monoplanes, preceding those of Hugo Junkers by some years, provide an example of one of the innovations attempted by other designers. Roger Sommer applied all-steel construction to a biplane. Although the appearance of his plane was fairly dated, the aeronautical press commented that the aircraft was far better finished than any of his other designs – the workmanship of which had generally been found wanting. Among all these innovations, the Short Brothers produced a monoplane of 'traditional' appearance.

The Germans already had their famous Rumpler–Etrich Taube monoplane by

this time, with its dated wing form. Although most Taubes were open-cockpit aircraft, cabin versions were built. Also, after its manufacture was undertaken by a number of other concerns in order to boost output, an all-steel version, the Stahltaube, appeared.

Not all of the effort was devoted to the aeroplane, even at a time when it was clearly the star of aeronautical progress. The year had opened with the ratification by the Aéro Club de France as a world

record distance for balloons the flight by Emile Dubonnet from Laymotte-Bruille to Sokolowska in Russia – a distance of 1953km 898m, or more than 1220 miles. This feat won for the intrepid balloonist the Lahm Cup for ballooning and an Aéro Club de France gold medal.

In the United States on 1 March, Captain Albert Berry, U.S. Army, made a parachute jump at St Louis from a Benoist biplane flown by Anthony Janners: '. . . . when a height of 1500 feet had been reached the airman steadied the biplane and Captain Berry let himself down through the frame. He then caught both of the rings of the parachute, which are attached to the aeroplane, let go, and dropped 300 feet before the parachute opened. He then drifted slowly to the ground.'

The novelty had not yet worn off flights across the English Channel. A 70hp Royal Navy Deperdussin monoplane was flown from Paris to Eastchurch,

FARMAN

AEROPLANE
BIPLANES
MONOPLANES

Ask for the 1912 Catalogue together with the Booklet, "How to Become an Aviator."

A.ply: 167 Rue de Silly-BILLANCOURT (Seine)

Telegrams: FARMOTORS-BILLANCOURT-SEINE.

Competition was forcing manufacturers to advertise – but there is still something of the early pioneer days about this Henri Farman advertisement which could offer a booklet on 'How to become an Aviator'.

Yes, your Short aeroplane will actually take-off; still the air of uncertainty lingers on into 1912.

non-stop, in just six hours on Saturday, 12 April by Maurice Prévost, with the London manager of British Deperdussin, D. Laurence Santoin, as a passenger. The aircraft apparently arrived in good shape after what was still a notable achievement, as it was flown that same evening by enthusiastic naval airmen.

But one of the most daring cross-Channel flights of the pre-World War I period must have been that of the then Chief Instructor at the Blériot Flying School at Hendon, Henri Salnet, hailed by the aeronautical press of the time as 'a second Védrines', and no wonder ! Salnet's ambition was to fly across the Channel both ways in one day. He flew from Hendon, to the north-west of London, to Issy-les-Moulineaux in just 3 hours 16 minutes – or a mere 2 hours 46 minutes if one discounts the 13 minutes spent

climbing over Eastbourne and the 17 minutes spent circling over Gisons to ascertain his position. This time was achieved because he made the first flight across the widest part of the Channel, between Eastbourne and Dieppe, following the most direct London to Paris route.

Salnet attempted to make the return journey that same day, starting at 2.15pm, but strong headwinds and heavy rain forced him down at Berck Plage at 5.55pm. He made the return cross-Channel flight the following day, but again had to interrupt his flight at Chatham because of dense fog. Salnet described his feat in laconic terms: 'For some time past I have wanted to fly to Paris and back in one day, and also, I should like to see M. Blériot in Paris

about some business matters.'

The other notable cross-Channel flight of 1912 was the first by a woman, the American Harriet Quimby, who flew from Deal to Cap Gris-Nez in a Blériot monoplane.

Although Glenn Curtiss had converted a seaplane into the first flying-boat in 1911, this had been a far from practical machine. In 1912, however, by further refining his basic design, he was able to build the first practical flying-boat. This offered greater promise of sturdy construction than the frail seaplane (or 'floatplane' as it was then called – Winston Churchill had still to coin the now accepted term for this type of aircraft and both floatplanes and flying-boats were more commonly known as hydro-aeroplanes). It was on a Curtiss hydro-aeroplane that Laurence Sperry successfully demonstrated the first rudimentary automatic pilot at Hammondsport, on Lake Keuka in New York State, in 1912.

The French designer, Denhout, designed and built his successful Donnet–Leveque flying-boat during 1912. A pusher-propeller biplane with the tailplane mounted on booms, one of the Donnet–Leveque's claims to fame, apart from its purchase by a number of air arms, was the introduction of the stepped hull into flying-boat design. This may have prompted Curtiss to build another flying-boat by the end of the year, one with a long hull and a tailplane aft of the mainplane. He also built a primitive amphibian, converted from his standard hydro-aeroplane, but with fixed landing wheels.

The United States Navy was making a number of experiments in catapult launching with its Curtiss hydro-aeroplanes. To start with, an overhead wire apparatus was used not unlike that employed by Stringfellow and Henson 70 years earlier. A real advance came when Captain Irvin Chambers, U.S.N., designed the first compressed-air catapult. Fitted onto a converted barge in the Washington Navy Yard, this enabled Lieutenant T. Ellyson, U.S.N., to fly a Curtiss A-1 'Hydro-aeroplane' from it on 12 November 1912. Subsequently, the invention of catapults meant that major warships could carry aircraft; battleships would normally carry three hydro-aeroplanes and cruisers two.

Such was the progress of the early hydro-aeroplane that, at Monaco in March 1912, the organisers of a power-boat meeting were able to add an event for hydro-aeroplanes to their programme. Most of the aircraft which appeared were conversions of landplanes.

The 1912 Naval Review, held in early May off Portland, saw the Royal Navy providing some of the most effective early demonstrations of the uses of air power – although in August the British Army was also to display the aeroplane and airship to good advantage. It was not surprising perhaps that this was also the year in which King George V accepted the Royal Aero Club's invitation to be-

An Antoinette mono-
plane being flown by
Hubert Latham at
Brooklands, near
Woking in England.
Before World War I
and between the wars,
Brooklands was
better known as a
racing-circuit than
as a flying ground.

come its patron.

Four of the Royal Navy's aircraft were taken to Portland: the Deperdussin, a Nieuport and two Short biplanes. One of the latter was converted into a workable hydro-aeroplane by the addition of three torpedo-shaped floats and was named 'H.M.S. *Amphibian*'. The battleship H.M.S. *Hibernia*, with a ramp constructed over her forecastle for launching the aircraft, was known as a hydro-aeroplane mother vessel!

Flying started with Samson leaving the boat-slip at Portland in 'H.M.S. *Amphibian*', taking-off and flying over the fleet while it lay at anchor. Other flights followed, with the recently pro-

moted Captain Gerrard, R.M.L.I., carrying a lady passenger, to the delight of the onlookers and the crews of the assembled ships. The passenger was none other than the daughter of the commander-in-chief, Admiral Callaghan. Flights were also made by Lieutenant Grey in both the Nieuport and Deperdussin monoplanes, and by Longmore in the other S.27.

During the Review, Samson's aircraft was used to carry a messenger for King George V. It landed alongside the Royal Yacht, *Victoria and Albert*, and the messenger was taken off in a dinghy. At this moment, Lieutenant Grey, R.N., flew past the *Victoria and Albert* at 500 feet and dropped a 300lb dummy bomb

The American-born, naturalized-Briton, Samuel Franklin Cody in his prime. This photograph was taken in late 1912, after his success in the Larkhill Trials, and the small insert is probably the Larkhill biplane, on which Cody was to meet his death in 1913.

from a safe distance before flying on past the battleship H.M.S. *Neptune*. Here he caused considerable alarm amongst those present by suddenly diving, only to pull out some 20 feet above the water – far from being in any difficulty, he had merely spotted a submarine, fortunately friendly, at periscope depth!

Serious aeronautical progress was probably best demonstrated at the Review by Samson's flight from the ramp on H.M.S. *Hibernia* while she steamed ahead at $10\frac{1}{2}$ knots in Weymouth Bay. This was the first flight from a ship underway. His Majesty was sufficiently impressed to include Samson amongst the officers invited to dine with him at the close of the Review. Not given to overstatement, Samson said about the efforts of the naval airmen at the Review: 'Good, good, but we shall do better.'

The United States Army, meanwhile, was taking delivery of five new Wright aeroplanes, and the French Navy took delivery of its first aircraft, a Maurice Farman biplane, in August. The potential of the aeroplane was not being overlooked by any of the major powers, although the Americans were beginning to lose some of their earlier momentum.

The French were the first to convert a

warship permanently to aircraft carrying. They converted the cruiser, *La Foudre*, late in 1912 to act as a seaplane carrier. By the time she rejoined the fleet the Royal Navy had opened the first of a chain of seaplane stations on the Isle of Grain to help defend England's East Coast. This was a pet project of the First Lord of the Admiralty, who at that time was none other than Winston Churchill. In contrast the Americans were becoming lukewarm in their attitude to aviation's defence possibilities. Their first seaplane station, at Guantanamo in Cuba, closed early in 1913 after being open only a few months.

An idea of the strength of the political driving force behind the French interest in military and naval aviation can be seen in the fact that official plans for a force of more than 200 aircraft were strongly criticised by politicians who firmly believed that France should have at least 400 aircraft!

French investment in strong aerial defences was dictated by events, and was not merely the result of militarism or jingoism. The intentions of her neighbour, Germany, over the Franco–German frontier were questionable. German airships continued to stray over the border, often landing on the pretext of technical trouble or claiming that they were forced down by inclement weather. Many French politicians and army officers who had previously suspected that the Germans were carrying out a military intelligence operation, were now convinced of it. The Germans were now combining their earlier devotion to the airship with a sudden interest in aeroplane development.

The French were not the only people to be disturbed by the size and quality of German air power. In October, the airship L.1, under the command of Count Ferdinand von Zeppelin himself, made a record 1000-mile flight. It left its base at Friedrichshafen at 8.35am on Sunday, 13 October, and arrived back at Johannisthal, near Berlin, at 3.43pm on Monday, 14 October. The near round-trip raised a considerable outcry in England as the result of a claim that the L.1 had been heard over Sheerness during the night of its epic voyage. In fact, nobody had actually seen the L.1, they only thought that they had heard it, but that didn't stop questions being asked in Parliament which could not be answered adequately by His Majesty's Ministers. And fears were not dispelled by Von Zeppelin's statement that he had at no time during the voyage approached the shores of England.

The British themselves had been far from idle, however, in developing national air power. In an attempt to improve the efficiency of military and naval aviation, the two air arms had been merged into the Royal Flying Corps in April 1912. In

Another tractor bi-plane from Shorts – the S.45 – with the novel feature of a single float, always a rarity on British designs although fairly common on inter-war period U.S. designs.

effect, this was the world's first air force, although its raison d'être was primarily linked to the needs of the Army. The R.F.C. had given a good account of itself in trials at Larkhill, on Salisbury Plain, in August. During the trials a Cody machine with a 120hp Austro–Daimler engine carried away the first prize. In fact, the best performance at Larkhill was that of the Royal Aircraft Factory B.E.2, piloted by De Havilland, but this was disqualified because of its origins and because one of the judges was the Superintendent of the R.A.F., Mervyn O'Gorman. Another excellent display of British aeronautical prowess was soon to follow at Hendon in August.

The Avro cabin biplane was a new British plane and it was in this aircraft that Lieutenant Wilfred Parke, R.N., became the first pilot to perform a deliberate spin and demonstrate recovery of control. Flying at 600 feet on 25 August, with an R.F.C. observer, Parke pulled his aircraft back from a too-steep approach, causing it partially to stall before he started to spin. Attempting recovery, Parke failed at first, and was only 50 feet from the ground when he applied rudder against the spin and pulled the

aircraft out. Unlike Raynham the previous year, Parke had a clear recollection of his movements and was able to contribute significantly to the improvement of air safety by his efforts.

The decline of the monoplane meanwhile had, ironically, been accelerated by nothing less than Louis Blériot's own honesty and integrity. Early in March, he detected a fault in one of his monoplane designs, which could have led to an accident and promptly notified the British and French governments, his two main customers. The French immediately grounded Blériot monoplanes for modifications suggested by Blériot which would enable the wings to withstand a degree of negative g.

Loss of confidence in the monoplane concept which had been hovering in the background, now came to the fore. By the end of the year the Royal Flying Corps had grounded all of its monoplanes while a committee of enquiry investigated their safety – reputedly, Churchill tried to prevent this ban from applying to aircraft operated by the Naval Wing, but without success.

Extreme though this action sounds in retrospect, the British had been further

alarmed by two very bad accidents which led directly to the ban. Lieutenant Parke, R.N., was killed with his passenger Hardwick while flying at Wembley, and Edward Petre was killed while flying his Martin–Handasyde (later known as Martinsyde). Petre's accident occurred while he was attempting what would have been one of the more noteworthy aeronautical feats of the year: a non-stop flight from Brooklands, some 20 miles south-west of London, to Edinburgh. He had covered more than 250 miles when he crashed in Yorkshire. Petre was Martin Handasyde's chief pilot, and it is worth noting that even at this time he was still considered a very experienced pilot even though he had only qualified six months before his death!

Before these tragedies, Wilbur Wright died at the early age of forty-five. He did not die from a flying accident but of typhoid fever, at 3.35am on the morning of 30 May. *The Times* said it all:

There has thus passed away, at the early age of 45, the elder of the two brothers to whose patient industry we owe the modern aeroplane. It is true that the Wrights were the actual inventors neither of the gliding machine nor of the idea of applying to it the petrol-driven motor. But it was they who first, by experiment, refined the theory and control of the glider, endowed it with an engine, and then raised it to the dignity of a true flying machine.

This was just one of many tributes from all over the world.

The Wrights had, of course, been self-taught flyers, as were most of the pioneers. Now there was a recognised need for aircraft which could be used specifically by student pilots. The flying schools were using more or less standard machines and the Avro 504 of 1913 was intended at first to be a scout. By the end of 1912, the first true training aircraft had appeared, in the Maurice Farman Longhorn biplane. Its 70hp Renault engine was reliable and the aircraft's handling was fairly predictable. It was to be the 'school' for many of the World War I British and French aces. The establishment of a purpose-built, training aeroplane was a sign that flying was now recognised as an activity for more than the talented and daring few.

7
PREPARATION FOR BATTLE

Biplane ascendant, aerobatics, death of a pioneer, challenge to the French, multi-engined aircraft, the amphibian, seaplane carriers, military applications, law for flight, Cody, De Havilland, Védrines, Prévost, Sikorsky, Garros

'If you are looking for perfect safety you will do well to sit on a fence and watch the birds.'
Wilbur Wright
(*1901*)

French historians have called 1913 'La Glorieuse Année', and they have not been alone in presenting the last year of peace as being outstanding. It was the end of an era – some might argue, for the better; but in many ways it was also for the worse. In aeronautics, the year was full of achievement, with a return to the verve and excitement of earlier years. The year 1913 was not without its tragedies, but technical achievements were highlighted by displays of skill and courage.

For the intrepid, long-distance aviators it was an exceptional year. On 17 April, Gustav Hamel, accompanied by one Duprée, flew his two-seat Blériot monoplane from Dover to Cologne, a distance of 250 miles, in just over $4\frac{1}{4}$ hours. The flight must have been difficult for Hamel and his passenger; it was also an ordeal for those spectators who saw Hamel leave Dover at 12.40, and within five minutes disappear from view in heavy rain and thunder. Their anxiety could not be dispelled until the news came of the aviator's safe arrival at Cologne at 4.58pm.

Less successful was the sponsored attempt to cross the Atlantic by airship. On arrival at Las Palmas in the Canary Islands, a representative of the sponsor

Charles Weyman was one of the more experienced pilots; an American, he was never outstandingly successful. He tried to follow Chavez across the Alps, but was forced to turn back by the severe conditions, and he entered the Schneider Trophy contest in both 1913 and 1914, without success. He was popular with his fellow pilots, although never an idol of the masses.

notified the Governor that the flight could not proceed because of difficulties in obtaining adequate supplies of hydrogen and of being certain of good weather throughout the flight.

Two very long-distance aeroplane flights enjoyed rather more success. Jules Védrines in a Blériot flew from Nancy to Cairo, and Bonnier in a Nieuport flew from Paris to Cairo. Both of these journeys took place towards the end of the year. Védrines left Paris on 20 November and flew via Prague, Vienna, Belgrade, Sofia, Constantinople, where he rested for a fortnight, and Tripoli – a distance of 2500 miles. He arrived at his destination on 28 December. Bonnier left Paris shortly after his fellow-countryman, following more or less the same route except for the substitution of Budapest and Baghdad, but suffered a series of mishaps before arriving at Cairo on 14 January 1914, and then flying on to Alexandria.

Undoubtedly the most spectacular of all the 1913 flights was that of Roland Garros. He flew a Morane–Saulnier monoplane from Fréjus in France to Bizerta in North Africa on 23 September, making the first non-stop aeroplane crossing of the Mediterranean. According to a report in *The Times*:

The airman Roland Garros left the naval air station at Fréjus, near St. Raphael, at 5.52 this morning on a Morane–Saulnier aeroplane driven by a Gnome engine, his intention being to fly to Tunis, and landed at Bizerta, 500 miles away at a quarter to two. He passed over Sardinia and made no stop at Cagliari.

The friends of Garros did their best to dissuade him from attempting this long flight, but Garros, who in December, 1912, flew from Tunis to Sicily, refused to listen to them, and even declined the official services of the Ministry of Marine. In spite of this refusal, however, the Minister of Marine insisted that torpedo boats

Maurice Prevost, the air-speed record-setter and 1913 Schneider Trophy winner, in the cockpit of his Monocoque Deperdussin float-plane. In common with most of the other entrants, the Monocoque Deperdussin for the Schneider contest was a conversion from a landplane.

should follow Garros in his flight to Africa. The success of the flight is greeted here with the utmost enthusiasm as showing how far in advance of their competitors the French aeroplanes and engines still are.

Garros later left Bizerta for Tunis, but darkness forced him to land some 15 miles from the city. Nevertheless, the French Prime Minister sent him a telegram, congratulating him on his success and expressing pride in the triumph of the French aircraft industry. But the French were not to remain for long as leaders of

aeronautical technology, in spite of their successes.

The British aircraft industry and its designers were already beginning to show what they could do, and many of their ideas were very sound indeed. The developed Farnborough B.E.2c and the new B.S.2 (later the S.E.2 fighter) were direct forerunners of the fighter aircraft of World War I. Private enterprise produced the small, but exceptionally manoeuvrable and fast, Sopwith Tabloid. This was fitted with an 80hp Gnome rotary engine, which gave it a maximum speed of 92mph and a rate of climb far in excess of that of

One of the early American aircraft to adopt the tractor biplane configuration was this Burgess floatplane, designed with the aid of Glenn Curtiss. This particular aircraft was sold to the U.S. Army in October 1913.

any contemporary monoplane. Less illustrious, but undoubtedly another of the great aircraft of the immediate pre-war and wartime period was the Avro 504, which also appeared for the first time in 1913. The Avro was intended as a scout at first, until it was realised that its maximum speed of just 80mph and its other attributes made it an ideal advanced trainer.

An unconventional aircraft, the Dunne No. 8, swept-wing and tail-less, proved to be very successful, flying from Eastchurch to Paris in August. Although the potential of the Dunne was never to be fully realised, if the potential for tailless aircraft generally has ever been realised, even today – by the end of the year the French firm of Nieuport had started to build the Dunne aircraft under licence. This was a turning of the tables indeed!

However, the French were still taking the honours. The Monocoque Deperdussin reappeared with a new and more powerful 160mph Gnome engine. It had a new pilot, Maurice Prévost, since Jules Védrines had suffered injury in a number of accidents. On 17 June, the up-rated aircraft established its first record of 111.74mph. Later in the year, during the Reims aviation week, Prévost raised the record further. He flew the Monocoque Deperdussin to victory in the 1913 Gordon–Bennett Cup Race on 29 September. This time he set the record at 126.67mph, flying in a dead calm. The final record was achieved only two days after an earlier record of 119.25mph had been set during the qualifying heats for the race. French confidence and delight in their aeronautical skill could well be excused, for this one aircraft had raised the air speed record by no less than 50 per cent.

Possibly one of the most spectacular performances by the Monocoque Deperdussin had taken place earlier in the year, at the Monaco Hydro-aeroplane meeting of 3–17 April. In the previous year, the

Adolphe Pégoud in his Blériot before take-off, obviously in high spirits. One of the most daring men in a profession not designed for the cautious, Pégoud was a pioneer parachutist as well as a stunt flier and a racer.

meeting had been tacked on to one concerned with power boats, but the hydro-aeroplane meeting of 1913 was an event on its own. The first Schneider Trophy race, which was not only to become an event on its own but to outlast all other aeronautical sporting events, was added to the Monaco meeting more or less as an afterthought.

The Schneider contest was primarily one between floatplane conversions of landplanes. Roland Garros and Dr Gabriel Espanet of France flew respectively Morane–Saulnier and Nieuport monoplanes; the latter type was also the mount of the American, Charles Weyman. The race was won in grand style by Maurice Prévost. At least, he thought that he had won it, but he had misread the rules and taxied across the finishing line instead of flying over it! Scared of losing the race to Weyman, Prévost argued over the decision, but when Weyman was forced to retire from the race, Prévost decided that it might be worth his while flying a final lap to secure his victory. He did so and won the race, but the time spent in argument and in flying the extra lap reduced his average speed from 61 to 45mph.

Another achievement for French design, and for the monoplane, at a time when both were being challenged, was the first flight over the Bernese Alps by a Blériot monoplane. The pilot was a Swiss, Oskar Bider. Bider had previously flown his aircraft over the Pyrenees and, in marked contrast to poor Chavez, he was able to report that his flight across the Alps was no more difficult than his trans-Pyrenean trip.

Already there were definite signs that the authorities were clamping down on the airmen. In May, a twenty-year-old Belgian, Brindejonc des Moulineis, was charged at London's Bow Street Police Court with two offences under the Aerial Navigation Act; failing to notify the authorities of his intention to enter the United Kingdom from abroad by air, and flying over parts of the United Kingdom, including London, without first obtaining official permission to do so. He pleaded guilty, explaining that although he had flown throughout Europe during the previous year, including Spain, Holland, Belgium, France and England, he had not

heard of the Act, nor had he encountered anything like it abroad. The Court treated him leniently, with the full agreement of the prosecution, binding him over for 12 months in his own cognisance of 1000 francs.

The new Act marked the first step along the road to the international control of aerial navigation. It was necessary for the protection of the community – against lawbreakers and smugglers as well as from possible aerial attack. Even at this early stage the need to distinguish between friend and foe amongst those who might come by air had become apparent. In the United Kingdom, the maximum penalties for offences under the Act were a £200 fine and six months' imprisonment.

Today, the 1930s are probably regarded as the great era of popular flying in Europe. However, it should be noted that in early 1913, Grahame-White produced a 'popular' biplane for less than £400, which compared favourably in many respects with the standard £1000 machine used by most aviators. The authorities were doing no more than their duty in

Short S.45 biplane in its more usual land-plane form.

paying regard to safety in the light of such attempts to extend the market for the aeroplane.

The French authorities were being no less strict with regard to aviation safety. No less a pioneer than Pégoud, one of France's leading and most experienced aeronauts, was forbidden to make a parachute descent from an aeroplane. However, on Wednesday, 20 August, he succeeded in 'eluding the vigilance of the authorities', according to one report, 'who had forbidden the trial on account of its dangers'.

The Times reported that:

The parachute, which is the invention of a canteen keeper named Bonnet, is folded in a box in the back of the body of the machine and is attached by ropes to the person of the airman. Pégoud was flying at a height of about 650 feet when he tested the parachute. He turned the machine downwards and released the parachute from its cover, whereupon it at once spread out and drifted slowly to the ground with its passenger. His aeroplane, the motor of which had been stopped, went through a series of fantastic movements before coming to earth, which it did without damage. Bonnet intends to construct a parachute capable of saving the aeroplane as well as its pilot from disaster in cases of accident.

On 13 May 1913, Igor Sikorsky's 'Bolshoi' ('Grand') made its maiden flight as the world's first four-engined aircraft; and with an enclosed cabin for captain and co-pilot, it proved to be well ahead of its time in every way.

On 6 September, a young sapper-aviator, Chanteloup, who was in the middle of his military service, having been a pilot for the Caudron company, to which he later returned, looped the loop, and was given a 15-day prison sentence by the military authorities.

Aerobatics had come to stay. Aircraft were even being built with this sport in mind. One of these was the Wright E biplane, which differed from its predecessors in having a single pusher-propeller while the tailplane was mounted on booms. The landing skids of the 'E' were built upwards and forwards in a manner similar to those of the Longhorn.

The loop had first been performed on 20 August 1913, by Lieutenant Nesterov of the Imperial Russian Army in a Nieuport monoplane. Adolphe Pégoud, the parachutist, was the first to fly in inverted flight for any length of time,

which he did on 21 September at Buc, in between flying two half loops. Pégoud had taken a number of precautions first, including strapping himself into his Blériot monoplane, which he had placed upside down on trestles, for up to 20 minutes at a time. The first Briton to perform the loop was B.C. Hucks, in September 1913. A contemporary account of Pégoud looping the loop at Brooklands, on 25 September, after taking off at 4.45pm comes from *The Times*:

He then climbed to about 4,500 feet, and at 5.5, amid a great silence, climbed until he was again inverted, and in this attitude performed a spiral vol plané, concluding with an 'S' as before. On this occasion he must have been lying head downwards for nearly three-quarters of a minute. Recovering his height, he climbed again for a few minutes, then the machine dived, carried on, stood up on its tail, carried on upside down, and climbed again, completing the full circle.

This was a small part of an exciting and successful performance. The excitement and the danger often extended beyond the risk to the airman, however, to threaten those on the ground as well. That the spectators enjoyed the thrills and spills, there can be no doubt, but there were those who saw the dangers clearly. When, on Saturday, 20 August, at the second Hendon Aerial Derby, an accident occurred to a 110hp Anzani-engined Champel flown by Mr Sidney Pickles with a Mrs Stokes as a passenger, at least one member of the public picked up his pen and wrote to *The Times*. According to Mr F.J. Nolan:

Cody's best known biplane, his so-called Larkhill biplane. This really only came second at the Larkhill trials, since the first prize could not be awarded to the best aircraft, a de Havilland, because one of the judges came from the Royal Aircraft Factory, where it was built.

A Renault 80hp engine, as used by the Burgess tractor biplane, and other designs of the period. It was not unusual for several different engines to be offered for any particular aircraft.

Mr Pickles' machine fell where a short time before crowds of spectators had assembled. Providentially, the spot where the aeroplane fell was clear at the moment, but the worry, none the less, is one that must not be passed by. Whenever flying is in progress at Hendon aviators must not only fly at dangerously low altitude over the enclosures, but also indulge in evolutions over the heads of the spectators which though they add to the 'thrills' of flying, should be sternly discouraged. That the officials of the Royal Aero Club and the Aerodrome are well aware of these dangers is proved by the fact that a rule exists forbidding airmen from flying over the enclosures. For some time this rule was observed, but it is now persistently ignored. It is surely imperative that the officials should take immediate action to stop this practice definitely, or that the police intervene, as they would do to stop any other public performance at which the most obvious and reasonable precautions to safeguard the spectators were disregarded.

Both Mr Pickles and Mrs Stokes were seriously injured in the accident.

The day after the Pickles and Stokes accident, Henri Farman crashed while flying one of his own aircraft at Etampes with his wife as a passenger. Descending in a spiral before landing, his machine went out of control at 150 feet, injuring

The British Army airship, Delta.

Farman, though not seriously, and his wife.

But the worst of the series of accidents which so bedevilled aeronautics that summer was undoubtedly the one which killed S.F. Cody and his passenger, W.H.B. Evans the cricketer. While flying at Laffan's Plain on 7 August Cody's aircraft – the same one which had performed so well at Larkhill a year before – disintegrated in mid-air. A popular figure in his adopted country, Cody's heroism and his devotion to flying, not to mention his flair, had earned him a place in aeronautical history more important, perhaps, than those of others who had made more worthwhile technical contributions. A contemporary account of his funeral described the large crowds, many deep, which lined the $2\frac{1}{2}$ mile route from North Camp Station, near Aldershot, to the military cemetery, while the gun carriage bearing the coffin was escorted by pipers of the Black Watch. At the time of his death Cody was 51 years old, although flying was generally regarded as a young man's sport. A fund was raised for his wife, to which the Royal Family contributed.

The aeroplane remained at the fore-front of military and naval developments. The early part of the year saw the French cruiser, *La Foudre*, which had been converted to act as a seaplane carrier late in 1912, undergoing trials. The Royal Navy converted the cruiser H.M.S. *Hermes* for the same purposes, carrying the new Short Folder biplane with backward folding wings to facilitate stowage on board ship. These were the first ships to undergo major conversion to carry aircraft as a part of their normal duties, although American and Japanese warships were to follow. In 1914 the *Hermes* was to be converted back to her old form – but not before a converted packet steamer joined the fleet in her place.

On the other side, the German Navy and the German Military Aviation Service were busily putting still more Zeppelins into service, as well as Rumpler-Etrich Taubes, Euler biplanes and licence-built Farman designs. Flying competitions were held, with the award of contracts to the most promising designs, to ensure a high standard of aircraft design for the armed forces.

British Army manoeuvres in Northamptonshire during September saw the opposing forces, 'White' and 'Brown',

Another notable engine, the Le Rhone 80hp.

using aircraft and airstrips for reconnaissance. Mock battles and attacks on airships by aircraft were also practised.

One of the two outstanding technical developments of 1913 was the first amphibian with a retractable undercarriage, the Sopwith 'Bat Boat'. The 'Bat Boat' was powered by a 90hp Daimler engine, and followed the flying-boat trend towards the stepped hull. The other development was the first flight of a four-engined aircraft on 13 May, when Igor Sikorsky, Russia's leading designer, flew his Bolshoi ('Grand'). The emergence of this machine indicated a great leap forward in aircraft design; the cabin was fully glazed, and interior fittings including a sofa, armchairs and a table, and there was cabin accommodation provided for the pilot and co-pilot, a feature which put the aircraft almost 21 years ahead of its time. Four 100hp Anzani engines gave the Bolshoi a cruising speed of 65mph, and by all accounts the aircraft flew and handled well. This was not only Sikorsky's first significant aircraft, but

also the first design with any promise by a Russian. In the years ahead Sikorsky was to prove, in the United States, that this early success was well deserved.

Dirigible progress continued, of course, even in Britain, although this country still lagged behind its European neighbours. A new dirigible, the Eta, was delivered to the British Army in August for its acceptance trials. One of these included towing the smaller Navy Airship No. 2, built by Willows, from Odiham to the Royal Aircraft Factory at Farnborough. This was an unusual exercise although it presented few problems in practice; the No. 2 was towed on a lower level than the Eta at the end of a 600-foot tow-line to minimise the risk of collision.

But all was far from well with British

airship progress, and even such unusual and spectacular tests as the towing operation could not really disguise this fact. The First Sea Lord, Admiral of the Fleet Lord 'Jackie' Fisher was concerned, and in an attempt to put an adequate airship for the Royal Navy into production quickly the device was hit upon of marrying a B.E.2c fuselage and engine to a dirigible envelope. Not satisfied with this, the Admiralty sent a delegation to Italy to observe the trials of the new Forlanini airship, and in 1914 Armstrong–Whitworth were asked to build one of these craft under licence.

Progress continued on other aeronautical fronts – including the attempts to solve the problems of night flying. One solution tried in 1913 consisted of fitting two rows of electric lamps to the leading edges of both wings on a Henri Farman biplane. Such a cumbersome method held no practical promise but the trials at Hendon proceeded without undue incident.

The year closed with the distance record being set by A. Seguin, who flew 634.54 miles in his Henri Farman over a closed circuit at Bruc. The altitude record of 20,079 feet was claimed by G. Legagneux in a Nieuport monoplane at St Raphael. These achievements served to maintain French pride and self-confidence, although they also did the French a disservice in enabling them to ignore signs of threats to their supremacy in the air – threats which were to become stronger in the year to come.

The Sopwith Tabloid landplane made its first appearance in 1913.

8
TIME TO GROW UP

Biplane triumph, the airbus, airlines and airships, trans-Atlantic flight, ready for battle, Curtiss, Sikorsky, Wright, Pixton

'It would be foolhardy. Machines as they are now constructed have not the staying power for a voyage of this length. In no circumstances would the engines hold out under the continuous stress of such a journey.'

Orville Wright
(*1914*)

Victor of the 1914 Schneider Trophy contest, the Sopwith Tabloid biplane effectively signalled the biplane's revival and rise to fame. It also paved the way for a brilliant series of World War I fighters.

One of the best known fliers of his day, Roland Garros in his Morane–Saulnier monoplane, with friend.

A glance at the notice board in the Royal Aero Club at the beginning of August 1914 would have seen the following notice to the membership from the then Chairman, the Marquess of Tullibardine:

Owing to the grave state of affairs on the Continent, it is possible that the British Empire may be involved in a European War. In such an event, the assistance of every able-bodied man might be required, and it is felt that no class of the community could be of more use to the naval and military authorities than the 'flying men'. The Royal Aero Club desires, therefore, to draw up a list of those aviators who, in the event of grave national emergency, might be prepared to offer their services. Names and particulars of aeroplane owned (if any) to the Royal Aero Club, 166, Piccadilly, London, W. Such a list would not be regarded as official or binding upon anyone, but would be retained in the club so that the information could be readily available in case of emergency.

This was not a moment too soon, for on 4 August the British Empire declared war on Germany and the aeroplane was to play a vital part in warfare for the first time. On the outbreak of war, 3000 men, all fully qualified, applied to join the Royal Naval Air Service, which had been formed in the July to provide the fleet with its own cover. The Admiralty was forced to announce hastily that it had more candidates than it needed.

To describe the first half of 1914 as the calm before the storm would be to exaggerate for, in the face of increasing international tension, the aeronauts took part in a final burst of activity. This included flying displays, as well as such new technical developments as an even larger Sikorsky, and the success of a biplane in the year's Schneider Trophy contest. Military aviation continued to make steady progress with an eye to the coming conflict. In reality the major powers had been moving, willingly or not, towards a major war for a decade.

There were no attempts on the airspeed record in 1914, and the 1913 record stood for the duration of the war, or at least it did so officially if not in practice.

The main speed event of the year was the Schneider Trophy contest, staged by the French as victors of the previous year. It was again held at Monaco, on Saturday, 18 April. On this occasion the true importance of the contest was recognised and it attracted competitors not only from France, but from the United Kingdom, the United States and Germany and Switzerland. In fact, not all of these actually succeeded in competing and some of those who did had to borrow

More than half the aircraft in the German Military Air Service at the outbreak of war were Rumpler Etrich Taubes of one kind or another – frequently built by other manufacturers, with many modifications. This is a standard machine at Paris in 1914.

aircraft because of the state of their own!

Competing against no less an aircraft than the 160hp Monocoque Deperdussin, as well as the similarly powered Nieuport and Morane–Saulnier, and pilots of the calibre of Espanet, Garros and Weyman, the Englishman, Howard Pixton, in his 100hp Gnome Monosoupape-powered Sopwith Tabloid biplane won the Schneider Trophy at an average speed of 86.78mph. He went on to set a 300km speed record for hydro-aeroplanes of 86.6mph, before landing in a rough sea. The performance of this small aeroplane – particularly its combination of manoeuvrability and speed – impressed and stunned the French, who had been confident of an easy victory.

Such was the general enthusiasm for aeronautical development that the *Daily Mail* was prompted to offer a £10,000 prize for the first trans-Atlantic flight. This was greeted with delight by many airmen and designers, but the war inter-

In 1914, Glenn Curtiss modified the Langley Aerodrome A in a last-ditch attempt to discredit the Wright patents – he failed. This is the modified aircraft in the air, with Curtiss in the pilot's seat.

Centre, below:
During the four years before the outbreak of World War I, Germany had built up a considerable civil and military Zeppelin airship fleet – carrying 35,000 passengers within Germany without incident.

A Short Folder seaplane, showing how aptly the aircraft was named, being lifted aboard H.M.S. *Ark Royal*, the collier converted to a seaplane carrier in 1914.

vened and the first flights did not take place until 1919. It is interesting to note that at this time one aeronautical journal was describing a young and still relatively unknown pilot as 'one of the steadiest of our young pilots'; he was John Alcock.

Glenn Curtiss, with the help of a retired Royal Navy officer, Lieutenant Commander J.C. Porte, designed and built his flying-boat 'America' in 1914. He intended to attempt the trans-Atlantic crossing with this twin-engined aircraft, sometimes known as the Curtiss-Porte. War prevented him, and the aircraft was sold to the British, becoming the forerunner of many British and American maritime-reconnaissance flying-boat designs.

Before leaving for the United States to work with Curtiss, Porte had been connected with the Supermarine Pemberton-Billing flying-boat, a remarkably futuristic design exhibited at the 1914 Aeronautical Exhibition at Olympia. The streamlining of the Pemberton-Billing was just one of its novel features, but this had to give way to less exciting but more practical craft in due course. It was on a Curtiss flying-boat in this year that Lawrence Sperry successfully demonstrated his new gyroscopic stabiliser

Orville Wright viewed the interest in a trans-Atlantic flight with well justified dismay, commenting that: 'It would be foolhardy. Machines as they are now constructed have not the staying power for a voyage of this length. In no circumstances would the engines hold out under the continuous stress of such a journey.'

The Wright factory was still producing

worthwhile aircraft with the help of designers recruited by Orville. Its latest production in 1914 was a flying-boat, with the advanced feature of an alloy-covered hull, which was also stepped, and with a deep 'V' form.

Less happily, Orville won the last of the appeals against the earlier judgments on the Wright patents – and immediately demanded a royalty of 20 per cent on every aircraft sold in the United States. This put Curtiss alone in the position of having to find $50,000! This alarmed the aeronautical industry generally, although some took comfort in the thought that the Dunne designs had carefully avoided

techniques for their own.

The airship services, which had been operating in Germany since 1911, continued during the first half of 1914. It was only in 1914, however, that the British started seriously to plan airship services of their own, to link major British cities and also London with Paris. Again, war prevented anything from coming of this idea.

More ambitious was the experimental airline service operated over the 20 miles between St Petersburg and Tampa in Florida by P.E. Fansler. He provided a Benoist flying-boat, piloted by A. Jannus. This lasted only for a matter of weeks.

One aircraft appeared early in 1914

Below:
The German Zeppelin airships, LZ 11 (left) and LZ 17 (right) in their shed.

Bottom of page:
Soon destined to become an important scout aircraft, this is a Farman 'Longhorn' in early 1914 – the name 'Longhorn' came from the exaggerated sweep of the skids at the front of the aircraft.

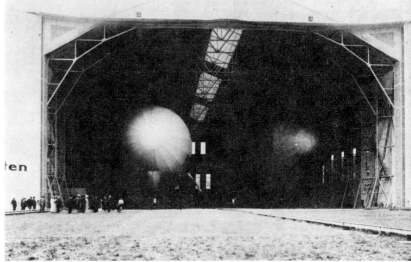

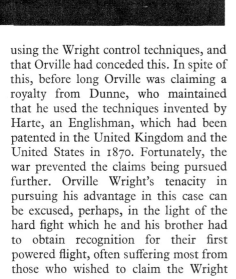

using the Wright control techniques, and that Orville had conceded this. In spite of this, before long Orville was claiming a royalty from Dunne, who maintained that he used the techniques invented by Harte, an Englishman, which had been patented in the United Kingdom and the United States in 1870. Fortunately, the war prevented the claims being pursued further. Orville Wright's tenacity in pursuing his advantage in this case can be excused, perhaps, in the light of the hard fight which he and his brother had to obtain recognition for their first powered flight, often suffering most from those who wished to claim the Wright

The prototype of yet another scout aeroplane of the war years, a Vickers 'Gunbus' in 1914.

which could have operated not only the American airline service, but the British and German airship routes as well. This was the second big Sikorsky aircraft, his Ilya Mourametz (meaning the 'Giant'), which first flew on 14 January. A development of the Bolshoi, the Ilya Mourametz was also a biplane with four 100hp engines, this time of Mercedes manufacture. The Ilya Mourametz was designed as an airliner. It carried no less than sixteen passengers for an 18 minute flight on 11 February, at an altitude of 300 metres – about 1000 feet. It performed the first of a number of long-distance flights a little later that same month, flying from St Petersburg to Tsarkoie-Selo and back. On this occasion a commentator actually described the aircraft as a giant 'airbus'!

By June, freed of the restraints of the long Russian winter, the Ilya Mourametz flew from St Petersburg to Kiev and back, making a number of stops – a flight of 2560 kilometres, or 1600 miles. Some people claim that it was on this flight that the first full meal was served in the air. This is open to debate, not only on the grounds of what constitutes a full meal but on exactly what sustenance the long-distance airship pioneers took with them. Undoubtedly the success of the Ilya Mourametz influenced Von Zeppelin to think in terms of larger aircraft, although he did little practical work until after the war. Almost eighty Ilya Mourametz aircraft were built during the war as heavy bombers, and performed well in this role.

In a climate of increasing international tension military aviation continued to develop as air arms were added to the armed forces of those countries which

had not already established them. Even in China, the government used aircraft to hunt a notorious bandit.

The United States found itself at war with Mexico early in the year. In April five Curtiss hydro-aeroplanes were used on reconnaissance duties against the Mexican port of Vera Cruz, flying from the battleship U.S.S. *Mississippi* and the cruiser U.S.S. *Birmingham*.

On its formation in July, the Royal Naval Air Service comprised fifty-two seaplanes and flying-boats, thirty-nine landplanes, seven airships and more than eight hundred officers and men.

In Japan, the naval transport *Wakamiya* was converted to act as a seaplane carrier.

In Germany new manufacturers appeared, including DFW – Deutsche Flugzug Werke. Commentators remarked on the tremendous strides being taken in Germany in aircraft production. Some of these aircraft were sold abroad, however, and an all-steel DFW biplane of the Royal Naval Air Service was able to fly from Gosport to Hull in May, taking just $7\frac{1}{2}$ hours in spite of heavy rain.

In Britain, apart from the conversion of vessels to act as seaplane carriers, and plans to put three seaplanes on battleships and two on cruisers for reconnaissance purposes, there were even more advanced plans. Most forward looking of all was the editor of *Flight*, who predicted that ships as small as destroyers would one day have their own aircraft! All in all, it was obvious when war was declared on 4 August between Britain and Germany, that the aeroplane would have to work hard for its living. It had made amazing progress in just eleven short years and now it was to be put to the test.

CONCLUSION

It is a widely accepted belief that the 1914–18 war advanced aviation more in four years than would have been possible in 40 years of peace. To accept this is to ignore not only the very real progress made between December 1903 and August 1914, but also the fact that the developments of World War I were made possible by stretching existing technology to its limits, rather than by any vast technological strides forward. For the most part engines and airframes were developments of designs available before the start of the war – with the possible exceptions of the Rolls-Royce in-line engines, but even these were developed from existing automobile engines.

Early in August, the German Military Aviation Service made the first bombing raid of the war on Paris. The following month the Royal Naval Air Service made an unsuccessful raid on balloon sheds at Düsseldorf. It was not until January 1915, that the first German Navy airship raid was mounted against an English town, Great Yarmouth.

Two significant developments of the war were the first landing of an aircraft on a ship underway, by Squadron Commander E.H. Dunning, R.N.A.S., who landed his Sopwith Pup biplane onto the forecastle of H.M.S. *Furious* on 2 August 1917; and the first take-off from a barge towed by a destroyer, by Commander Charles Rumney Samson who flew a Sopwith Camel from such a barge in July 1918. Unfortunately he crash-landed in the water after fouling part of the barge during take-off. On 1 August, Sub-Lieutenant Stuart Culley, R.N.A.S., made a successful barge take-off. Less happily, poor Dunning had been killed on 7 August 1917, while attempting to repeat his earlier achievement.

After the war, in August 1919, airline services were started between London and Paris using converted Airco D.H.4 bomber aircraft – soon supplemented by civil conversions of Farman, Vickers and Handley Page bombers. The newly founded Soviet Union suffered a setback in this field after Igor Sikorsky was forced to flee the Revolution to live and work in the United States.

Airships soon fell from favour in the United States and the United Kingdom, although the Germans persisted with them until the Hindenburg disaster of 1937. Count Ferdinand von Zeppelin was instrumental in encouraging the building of large airliners in Germany during the early 1930s, but few of these aircraft were successful. The highly successful Junkers and Focke-Wulf airliners did not appear until the end of the decade. More was achieved by the flying-boat, which did much to open up the world's long-distance air routes between the wars, although it was also assisted by such notable landplanes as the Junkers, Ford, and Fokker trimotors.

Throughout good years and bad the Schneider Trophy contest survived. The Trophy was won outright for Britain in 1931, by a Supermarine S.6B monoplane, which also took the world air-speed record. It thus justified Jacques Schneider's belief that the seaplane offered an ideal form for speed. Schneider himself had died in reduced circumstances some time before, and the difficulties of mounting the competition resulted in it being held only every other year after 1927.

There were other changes, too, in the conduct of the Schneider Trophy, for the post-war period saw the end of the private entry, and then the company entry, and finally only state support could ensure success. This was the sad side to aviation between the wars – the field became too big and too costly for the individual, and then for the company, to remain in the forefront of pioneering effort. The measure of success achieved increasingly bore a relationship to the amount of state support provided – a state of affairs which would have dismayed many of the early pioneers.

CHRONOLOGY

1903: **17 December**   First powered heavier-than-air flight by Orville Wright.

1904:   Esnault-Pelterie, Archdeacon and Ferber work on Wright-type gliders in France.
Cody experiments with man-lifting kites for the British Army.
  26 May   Wright Flyer II flies.
  7 September   Wrights start catapult take-offs.
  20 September   Wilbur Wright flies first circle.
  9 November   Wilbur Wright makes first flight of more than 5 minutes.

1905:   Voisin–Archdeacon and Voisin–Blériot float-gliders fly.
  16 March   Moloney flies Montgomery glider from balloon.
  June   Wright Flyer III flies.
  4 October   Orville Wright makes first flight of more than 30 minutes.
  14 October   F.A.I. formed.
  16 October   Wrights stop flying until 1908.

1906:   Wrights' patents granted.
  March   Vuia tractor monoplane tested, unsuccessfully.
  12 September   Ellehammer makes tethered hop flight of 140 feet.
  12 November   Alberto Santos-Dumont flies for 721 feet.

1907:   Phillips makes tentative flights in Britain.
Dunne tail-less, swept-wing biplane tested, without success.
Ellehammer conducts tests with triplane.
Voisin–Delagrange pusher-biplane tested, without success.
  29 September   Breguet man-carrying helicopter makes tethered flight.
  October   Henri Farman flies.
  November   Santos-Dumont No. 19 monoplane tested.
Blériot tests No. VII monoplane, with little success.
  10 November   Henri Farman flies for over one minute on a Voisin.
  13 November   Cornu helicopter makes man-carrying flight, untethered.

1908: **13 January**   Henri Farman flies first European circle at Issy-les-Moulineaux.
  6 May   Wright brothers resume flying with modified Flyer III.
  14 May   Wilbur Wright takes C.W. Furnas on first passenger flight.
  30 May   Farman takes Archdeacon on first European passenger flight.
Delagrange remains airborne in a Voisin for quarter of an hour.
  June   Roe tests his first biplane in England.
  28 June   Ellehammer flies in Germany.
  4 July   Curtiss wins *Scientific American* trophy for first public flight in the United States.
  8 August   Wilbur Wright flies in public at Hunaudières, France.
  3 September   Orville Wright flies in public at Fort Myer, at the start of his demonstrations for the U.S. Army.
  9 September   Orville Wright makes first flight of more than one hour.
  17 September   First fatal aeroplane accident, Lieutenant Selfridge is killed while flying as Orville's passenger.
  16 October   First British flight by S. F. Cody at Farnborough.
  31 December   Wilbur Wright makes first flight of more than two hours.

1909:	Weiss flies his bird-form gliders.
23 February	McCurdy makes first flight in Canada in his 'Silver Dart'.
March	Goupy II flies.
April	First aerial cinematograph shots from Wright A at Rome.
25 July	Louis Blériot flies English Channel from Calais to Dover.
27 July	Latham fails in his second cross-Channel flight attempt.
August	First aviation meeting held at Reims, in France, sponsored by champagne industry; first official air speed records.
27 August	Henri Farman makes first flight of 100 miles in just under three hours at Reims.
2 October	Orville Wright makes first flight at 1000 feet.
23 October	Mme Baroness de la Roche becomes first qualified woman pilot.

1910:	Coanda tests first jet-propelled aeroplane, without success.
	Zeppelin starts airship services within Germany.
February	Hugo Junkers granted patent for cantilever wing.
10 March	Aubrun makes first night flight, in a Blériot, in Argentina.
28 March	Fabre makes first hydro-aeroplane flights.
28 April	Night flight in England by Claude Grahame-White.
2 June	Hon. Charles Rolls makes first double crossing of the English Channel.
July	Curtiss makes first bombing trials in the United States.
12 July	Hon. Charles Rolls killed in flying accident at Bournemouth.
17 August	Moisant and his mechanic make first cross-Channel passenger flight in a Blériot.
27 August	McCurdy experiments with air-to-ground radio transmission while flying Curtiss biplane in the United States.
23 September	Chavez makes first trans-Alpine flight, but sustains fatal injuries from landing accident.
14 November	Lt. Eugene Ely, U.S.N., makes first take-off from a ship using a Curtiss biplane.

1911:	Wright brothers win first round of their battle over patents.
	Montgomery killed while flying one of his own gliders.
	Trial airmail flights.
January	Bombing trials in the United States at San Francisco. Curtiss tests first practical hydro-aeroplane. McCurdy flies for 90 miles over water from Key West to Havana.
18 January	Ely makes first landing on and take-off from a ship.
12 April	Prier makes first non-stop London to Paris flight.
August	Atwood makes St Louis–Chicago–New York flight.
3 August	Fabre–Voisin seaplane flies.
Sept–Nov	Calbraith Rodgers flies from Long Island to Long Beach in 82 days.
22 October	Italians use Blériot monoplane on reconnaissance duties against the Turkish Army.
24 October	Orville Wright makes record soaring flight of 9 minutes.
Oct–Nov	'Concours Militaire' at Reims.

1912: Royal Aircraft Factory B.S.1 flies, paving the way for the World War I fighting scout.

Curtiss flies first flying boat.

Avro flies first cabin biplane.

February	Védrines takes speed record over 100mph mark in the Monocoque Deperdussin.
1 March	Berry makes first parachute drop from an aeroplane in the United States.
March	First seaplane meeting a Monaco.
13 May	Royal Flying Corps comes into being.
August	Cody wins first British military aeroplane competition at Larkhill.
12 November	Chambers–Curtiss catapult launch, with Lt. Ellyson, U.S.N.

1913: Sopwith Tabloid, Royal Aircraft Factory B.E.2c, Avro 504, Dunne No. 8 flies.

Schneider Trophy contest inaugurated.

Sikorsky Bolshoi flies.

Wrights win appeals against the judgments on their patents.

20 August	Nesterov loops the loop for the first time, flying a Nieuport at Kiev.
September	Pégoud loops the loop in a Blériot.
23 September	Roland Garros makes first non-stop trans-Mediterranean flight.

1914: Fansler operates first trial airline service in the United States.

Sikorsky Ilya Mourametz flies.

World War I starts on 4 August.

GLOSSARY

aeroplane, airplane (US) a heavier-than-air powered flying machine.

aerostat a balloon or an airship, built for lighter-than-air flight.

aerostation the art or science of lighter-than-air flight.

aileron a flap-type device normally fitted to the trailing edge of the outer wing, or sometimes between the wings on an early biplane, which enables the pilot to bank an aircraft and provides some assistance in turning.

airship a powered, steerable lighter-than-air flying machine, either rigid (dirigible) or semi-rigid (semi-dirigible), the Germans and Americans usually favouring the former and the British the latter.

biplane an aeroplane with two sets of wings, one above the other to provide extra lift.

canard a tail-first aeroplane.

dirigible *see* airship, above.

floatplane as the name suggests, an aeroplane with floats instead of wheels.

flying-boat although also having floats, the flying-boat has its hull, part of the fuselage, also in the water.

monoplane an aeroplane with one set of wings.

tandem-wing an aeroplane with both the mainplane and tailplane of more or less the same size.

triplane an aeroplane with three sets of wings, one above the other.

PICTURE ACKNOWLEDGEMENTS

For permission to use the photographs on the pages listed below, the author would like to thank the following:

Crown Copyright, Imperial War Museum pages 114, 115, 150.

Science Museum pages 11, 13, 14, 16, 18, 20, 28, 43, 46, 53, 55, 69, 72, 74, 79, 80, 82, 86, 88, 103, 118, 119, 127, 128, 141, 142, 144.

Smithsonian Institution page 150.

Library of Congress pages 11, 12, 15, 23, 32, 33, 51, 59, 69, 75, 84, 85, 93, 98, 100, 101, 102, 137, 148.

Musée de l'Air pages 18, 26, 27, 29, 30, 31, 41, 49, 54, 56, 59, 60, 61, 62, 65, 67, 74, 134, 135, 136, 138, 149.

Bibliothèque Nationale pages 23, 49.

Royal Aeronautical Society pages 34, 35, 37, 38, 50, 53, 71, 79, 81, 86, 94, 95, 110, 111, 119, 129, 140, 150.

Royal Aircraft Establishment pages 21, 83, 88, 106, 109, 120, 122, 143.

Short Brothers Ltd pages 70, 104, 114, 139.

Hawker Siddeley Aviation pages 145, 148.

INDEX

Page numbers in italic type indicate captions to illustrations